The Pedagogy of African Languages

an emerging field

A publication of The Ohio State University
National East Asian Languages Resource Center

in cooperation with

The National African Language Resource Center
at the University of Wisconsin, Madison

funded by

The U. S. Department of Education

Pathways to Advanced Skills series, volume V
Series General Editor: Galal Walker

Distributed by The Ohio State University
Foreign Language Publications & Services Office

Executive Editor: Galal Walker
Managing Editor: Christopher Antonsen
Distributions Manager: Gregory Wilson
Editorial Assistants: Perry Miller & Kristal Coleman

Cover design: Kristina Emick
Layout: Chris Antonsen

The Pedagogy of African Languages

an emerging field

Antonia Folarin-Schleicher
Lioba Moshi

Pathways to Advanced Skills series, volume V

Published by
The National East Asian Languages Resource Center
The Ohio State University

in cooperation with
The National African Language Resource Center
University of Wisconsin, Madison

2000

This volume prepared and published by

National East Asian Languages Resource Center
The Ohio State University
276 Cunz Hall
1841 Millikin Road
Columbus, Ohio 43210

614-292-4361 • fax: 614-292-2682
www.flc.ohio-state.edu/nflrc/

Library of Congress Cataloging-in-Publication Data

Schleicher, Antonia Yétúndé Folárìn, 1953-
    The pedagogy of African languages : an emerging field / Antonia Y.
Folarin Schleicher, Lioba Moshi.
        p. cm. -- (Pathways to advanced skills series ; v. 5)
    "In cooperation with the National African Language Resource
Center, University of Wisconsin, Madison."
    Includes bibliographical references and index.
    ISBN 0-87415-174-0
    1. African languages--Study and teaching. 2. African languages--
Research. I. Moshi, Lioba J. II. Title. III. Series.

PL8004 q.S49 2000
496'.071--dc21
                                                        00-067617

Manufactured in the United States of America
Printed and bound by Cushing-Malloy, Inc., Ann Arbor, Michigan

ISBN 0-87415-174-0

This book is dedicated to our mothers: the late Mrs. Victoria Olufowora Folarin and the late Mrs. Marpha Nzarenau for instilling a sense of diligence and stick-to-it-iveness in us.

CONTENTS

ACKNOWLEDGEMENTS

The authors of this book would like to thank all of our colleagues and students who contributed one way or the other to the successful completion of *The Pedagogy of African Languages: An Emerging Field*. During the years spent writing this book, a number of the draft chapters were read and critiqued by graduate students in Schleicher's "African Language Teaching Methods: Theory and Practice" course at the University of Wisconsin-Madison. Versions of some of the chapters were also presented at different African Language Teachers Association (ALTA) annual meetings. The comments of our colleagues who were present at the different presentations, and of the students who took Schleicher's methods course, were very helpful in shaping the final revision of these chapters.

We are especially grateful to Chris Antonsen, Production Editor for the National East Asian Languages Resource Center, for his invaluable support during the development of this book. Thank you Chris for your sound suggestions and careful and creative editorial efforts.

We are also indebted to all of the editorial staff at the NEALRC, including Galal Walker, Series Executive Editor, who in conjunction with Chris Antonsen gave us the idea for this book; Kristina Emick, Cover Designer; and Krystal Coleman and Perry Miller, Editorial Assistants. The time and expertise of these people greatly contributed to the finalization of this manuscript.

Finally, we are thankful to the U. S. Department of Education Office of International Education whose funding made this book possible.

FOREWORD

The field of African languages is emerging with tremendous potential in the age of technology. With renewed American interests in study abroad programs, research, and leisure travel in Africa, this is a great opportunity for the field to reclaim a stature built by past and present scholars of African languages and linguistics. Like other fields, African language teaching has a very strong pedagogical orientation in its research and teaching traditions. This began in the latter part of the twentieth century and, without doubt, will gain strength in the twenty-first century and beyond.

The authors of this volume believe that now is the time for the field to show its strengths and achievements. The field was fairly obscure until 1991 when the African Language Teachers Association (ALTA) began its field development mission. With support from the National Council on Less Commonly Taught Languages (NCOLCTL), ALTA began an energetic course which has indeed invigorated the field. It prides itself with strong leadership, field projects organized by task forces which have been instrumental in the development of goal-based teaching and learning, the development of a teacher's manual for Swahili, the creation of an annual international conference, the publication of a journal (JALTA), and most recently the establishment of a National African Language Resource Center (NALRC) at the University of Wisconsin, Madison.

This book is one more watershed in the achievements of the field. It is intended to be the first in a series of publications that will report on field developments in language and culture teaching and research on language pedagogy. This book emphasizes the fact that language teaching and learning depend on knowledge about language, culture, communication strategies, and other learning strategies. It highlights the importance of field-based expertise with a wide knowledge base that includes specific language information and ability to apply the knowledge base to language instruction.

This book has eight chapters. Individually, each author focuses on specific issues and has written different chapters: Lioba Moshi wrote chapters one, three, and four and Antonia Folarin-Schleicher wrote chapters two, five, and six. Together, the authors used their expertise in materials development and teaching experiences to shape chapters seven and eight. Needless to say, the chapters are organized to show both cohesion and coherence in its entirety.

In chapter one, Moshi focuses on past and current developments in the field of African languages. She explores the rationale for development by looking at the field's structure (which includes the Title VI and non-Title VI centers) in advocating and providing leadership for the field. She also discusses the development of teaching materials. This theme is continued by Schleicher in chapter two in which she explores the state of African language instruction in the United States. She reports on a survey that was conducted in order to provide ALTA with an inventory of the state of academic programs, assets, and resources.

In chapter three, Moshi looks at teaching and focuses on the teacher and methods of teaching. She carries on in chapter four and focuses on learners and learning strategies exploited by students who choose to study African languages.

In chapter five, Schleicher expands on chapters three and four by advocating an approach to teaching—specifically "goal-based" instruction. Not only does she define and show how the approach can be utilized, but she also explores the rationale for such an approach in the teaching of African languages. In chapter six, she focuses on the development of cultural proficiency in African languages.

In chapter seven, Moshi and Schleicher display their field expertise and experiences in producing and teaching with video, CD-ROM, and other computer-assisted materials like WebCT and the World Wide Web. In chapter eight, they put forth their vision for the instruction of African languages in the twenty-first century by evaluating the benefits of ALTA as a field-linking tool and as an active voice for a marginalized field. They also explore (1) ALTA's role in the development of a national strategic plan and a sustainable national African Language Resource Center with a coherent mission, goals, and objectives; (2) meeting national needs and capacity; and, most of all, (3) the need to professionalize the field of African languages.

Moshi and Schleicher are convinced that this volume will not only introduce ALTA's field development success to the world but that it will also inspire other ALTA members to produce more publications collaboratively.

CHAPTER ONE

African Language Field Development

1. BACKGROUND

To understand the complexity of African language field development in the United States, we need to explore the structure of existing language programs. Basically, there are two types of institutional affiliation for African language programs: Title VI-center affiliated programs and non-Title VI affiliated programs (i.e., department/other unit). Consequently there is remarkable variation across institutions, a hallmark that distinguishes one African language program from another across the nation. Distinctions include the type and amount of resources available, teaching expertise, methodology, and program viability.

Depending on the type of affiliation, an African language program can be enhanced or left on a life-support system for a number of years with no chance for genuine development. At one level, a language program that is affiliated with a Title VI funded center will benefit both from the center's visibility at the local and national levels. Programming is greatly influenced and aided by the Title-VI center. The absence of such a powerful unit in a non-Title VI center creates immense challenges that are clearly reflected in how the language program is administered, sustained, and (most of all) if it can survive beyond its elementary stage offerings.

In many cases, non-Title VI affiliated programs reside in language, literature, or linguistics programs or departments. The development and ultimately the survival rate for such a program depends largely on the popularity of the language being taught at institutional as well as national levels.

Presently, the African languages taught in the United States fall into three categories (Dwyer and Wiley 1980[1]; Dwyer 1991)[2]: Group I languages which include the commonly taught African languages (Swahili, Hausa, Yoruba, Wolof, Zulu, Xhosa, Setswana, Amharic), Group II languages which include the less commonly taught African languages (such as Bamileke, Bemba, Ganda [also Luganda], Kikuyu, Mende, Tiv, to name only a few), and Group III languages which constitute the least commonly taught of these languages. Generally, group I languages may attract between 10 and 30 students (with Swahili leading this group by attracting more students), followed by Yoruba and Hausa. Group II may attract between five and 10 students while Group III is unpredictable, attracting fewer than five. Group III languages are, therefore, taught on demand from year to year.

---

1. cf. *African Language Instruction in the U.S.: Directions and Priority for the 1980s.* African Studies Center, Michigan State University.

2. cf. *Final Report of the Conference on African Language Teaching in the U.S.: Directions for the 1990s.* Kellogg Center, Michigan State University.

Without doubt, these groupings affect institutional motivation to support the development of a particular language. The motivation is often reflected in how the language program is administered, the selection and rewarding of instructors, and most of all the enthusiasm shown by students who select that language for various college credit requirements.

Within the Title VI-affiliated programs, institutional motivation is very different. The institution may have humanistic or cultural interests as the force behind their motivation for initiating, developing, and sustaining a particular language program. In contrast, the non-Title VI-affiliated programs, depend entirely on programming structures, administrative as well as instructional. It is the strength of the programming structure that makes or breaks any language program. The three most common administrative and instructional structures are:

A. faculty in charge of programming and instruction
B. faculty in charge of programming only
C. no faculty in charge of instruction or programming

The majority of Title VI-affiliated programs fall into categories A and B compared with about one percent of the non-Title VI programs that fall into category A and ten percent into category B. The placement of Title VI-affiliated programs squarely in category A can be explained as a consequence of their attempt to fulfill a requirement imposed by the Department of Education, the granting agency for Title VI centers. One of the requirements is the demonstration of a strong language program headed by a professional teacher, preferably a trained linguist. There are several advantages for programs with structures A and B: (1) credibility that is associated with faculty teaching the class; (2) a certain level of legitimacy associated with the fulfillment of a language requirement; (3) high local and national visibility, often associated with increased student enrollments as well as students' ability to participate in national programs such as the Department of Education Group Projects Abroad. Needless to say, types A and B enjoy much respect from students who prefer a program directed by a faculty member, and best of all a class taught by a faculty member rather than a teaching assistant or temporary staff.

As noted above, about ten percent of non-Title VI language programs fall into type B. Often the program may be characterized by the absence of well grounded program controls resulting from a weak relationship between the instructor and the managing unit (department, program or center). The faculty in charge will often reside in the same department as the language program, but his or her responsibilities are minimal, ranging from finding an instructor for the class, reporting grades, and advising students taking the language class. Issues of content, context, and methodology are left to the instructor regardless of whether the instructor is trained or untrained. The instructor may be selected based on the interests of the faculty in charge of programming. In many cases native language proficiency is taken as the major criterion, foregoing training and teaching experience. The pool from which the selection can be made includes potential graduate students, graduate students already at the institution, and native speakers in the community. Consequently, the academic background of the potential teacher could be anything but language and linguistics. Where the language is administered in a language or linguistics unit, the faculty in charge may provide in-service training to the instructor or co-teach with the instructor; however, if the teacher has no stakes (which is often the case where the academic background of the teacher is not relevant to his or her teaching a language class), such efforts may not bear lasting effects. This may also be affected by a lack of interest and commitment to excellent programming from the administering unit. It is not possible to find a motivated faculty member who would devote his or her research time developing and programming a language that is barely supported by the administering unit.

In category C we can place the remaining ninety percent of the African language programs in the non-Title VI institutions. As noted earlier, there is often no programmer or faculty in charge of instruction. In other words, the responsibility for programming and instruction is left solely to the language instructor, whether trained or untrained. Interestingly, such programs tend to have large enrollments in popular languages like Swahili and Yoruba. Surveys show that such institutions tend to have a sizable population of black students or are historically black colleges. The motivation to teach or learn an African language is largely cultural, and in most cases the encouragement originates from the administrative unit which in all likelihood is an African-American Studies program or a Black Studies Department where the curriculum focus has a historical, social, or cultural perspective concerning the continent of Africa. As noted earlier, the language choice may be influenced by individual interests, but most often it is influenced by the popularity of the three major languages (Swahili, Yoruba and Hausa) with Swahili rated higher than all possible choices.

2. RATIONALE FOR AFRICAN LANGUAGE DEVELOPMENT

The need for an African language at any campus and its consequent development are intricately linked to the institution's goals and also to the language program's goals and learner outcomes in the context of the available institutional learning resources. As noted earlier, the institutional base for the language determines the success of the program's development as well as its longevity. However, both the development and longevity can be greatly enhanced by the selected model of programming and instruction (cf. A-C, above). It also depends on the modes through which the language is taught. There are two traditional modes: (1) teacher-led and (2) tutorial. The teacher-led mode of instruction is popular for teaching the most commonly taught African languages (Group I) and to some extent some of those in Group II. These will be the languages likely to be offered annually, at the elementary and possibly intermediate levels. The teacher-led mode is very teacher-centered, with a typical class size of between 10 and 30. Tutorials, on the other hand, serve the less and least popular languages (Groups II and III) and may attract between two and five students at any level, with the highest number at the elementary and intermediate levels. They also attract more graduate students (based on language needs for research purposes) than undergraduates.

It is also used extensively at the advanced levels for all groups (I-III). Although the tutorial mode is considered learner-centered (the learner determines the structure, pace, and teacher's involvement), more often than not the tutorials are teacher-supervised for content and quality. Institutions tend to favor the teacher-led mode although one may find cases in which institutional goals, resources allocated, and other local conditions constitute the basis under which one language or another is selected for a tutorial-based instruction with open terms and conditions.

3. STRUCTURAL BENEFITS

As noted earlier, there are different institutional structures which may encourage or discourage the development of a strong African language program. The nature of support afforded will dictate the type of institutional linkages, valuation, interest, staffing, and perspectives for the language program.

3.1 Linkage

It is possible for a language program to have direct linkage to the most influential members of an institution (e.g., the dean, other unit heads). If that is the case, the ensuing relationship fosters development. The relationship between the head of a language unit, and the faculty/instructor in charge is also improved as a consequence of a clear chain of command that does not end at the head's desk but which has a chance to move up the ladder to where the resources are administered. This type of relationship, however, greatly depends on how the language program was established (as independent or dependent of the administering unit) because budgeting and distribution of resources is always a thorny issue in departments that administer language instruction. If the budget for the language program is a "micro-bite" of the overall budget of the administering unit, the rate of survival of the language program is low. On the other hand, if the language program was established independently of the administering unit and its budget is an addition to that of the administering unit, the rate of survival (all being equal) is higher, a rarity in many institutions. Needless to say, there are not many institutions in this enviable position. As noted earlier, program survival is best ensured where a faculty member is directly connected to the language program. Such a faculty member often possesses a rare determination to make the language program successful and worthwhile to the institution and the students.

Although unit-and inter disciplinary linkage are attainable in institutions with type B language program structure, it is relatively difficult to sustain. This can be explained by the fact that such programs are often established by and for interest groups that may or may not have much visibility in the overall structure of the institution. In such a case, they block the avenue through which a linkage between the instructor and the administering unit could be fostered. Likewise, the linkage between the unit head and other units that constitute the institutional constituencies will remain non-existent. Consequently, the language program's visibility will be confined to a small segment of the institution (its home base) and we cannot, therefore, expect much development and/or sustainability.

Because of the nature and motivation associated with language instruction in type C programs, there is always a good chance that the language program will develop a strong and close linkage with the administering unit. As noted earlier, the relationship and affinity are fostered through cultural motivation and, to some extent, historical factors. Granted that administering units may have more administrative freedom than perhaps a language, literature, or linguistic program or department, a direct linkage with the most influential members of the institution and those who control resources is often guaranteed. If the unit head has high stakes in the language program, the relationship between the instructor and the unit head develops very quickly and can become quite strong in a relatively short period. In most cases, the budget for the language program will be fully integrated in the fiscal budget of the unit. Consequently (all being equal), development, visibility, and the sustainability of the language program are ensured.

There is one additional observation regarding the environment for type C programs worth making: Despite the fact that a type C environment can be conducive to the development of a language program with more than one language, experience shows that institutions with type C programs have shown resistance to expansion and prefer programming that is simple and cost effective.

3.2 Valuation

Like linkage, how a language program is valued depends on whether it has a Title VI or non-Title VI affiliation. In most cases, the problem of undervaluation is not as critical in Title VI programs because of the strong linkage between Title VI and the language instruction administering unit. The unit ensures that the activities of the language program remains sustainable by providing for the language and by keeping an interest in maintaining the language to satisfy Title VI funding and continuation requirements. The pressure to prove to the institution that it is worthwhile to keep the program in the books lies more with non-Title VI-affiliated programs where there is pressure to maintain as well as to increase enrollments by keeping the students interested in the language. Interestingly, enrollments in most of the type C instructional programs is not a problem at the elementary levels because the motivation has remained largely cultural and, for a small minority, only to satisfy a language requirement.

3.3 Interest

To plan for the development of African languages in the United States, one must first assess the level of interest in the teaching and learning of these languages. The interest shown in the teaching and the learning of African languages is at best mixed and greatly dependent on the type of unit affiliation the language program enjoys at the institution. It also depends on the type of instruction available (types A-C). Most critically, it depends on the institution's commitment to the development of the program. Institutional support from the deans and head of department will serve as the main force behind a steady growth of interest among students and faculty in the home department. Institutional support often enhances the program's attempts to secure linkages with other units, departments, or programs. Likely targets include history, geography, political science, anthropology, sociology, comparative literature, and music departments. The interest is most often guaranteed where these subjects are taught by an African or Africanist. Additional visibility could bring in students from less likely units like the sciences, medicine, ecology, journalism, and religion departments. Where what is proposed here has been tried, evidence shows that interest has crossed out of the boundaries of humanities and into the sciences, particularly biology, environmental science, ecology, agronomy, applied agricultural economics, medicine (including pharmacy), and education. Surprisingly, African languages have not been able to influence language education departments which are over-whelmingly interested in ESL and the more commonly taught languages (German, French, and Spanish).

3.4 Staffing

Less than ten percent of the institutions which offer African languages have full-time tenured or tenure-track faculty members teaching language. Interestingly, non-Title VI-affiliated programs do have full-time, tenured or tenure-track faculty teaching African languages. This is a consequence of the fact that many non-Title VI-affiliated programs were established with the full support of their institutions rather than as a consequence of soft money received from a major grant. With institutional support comes the intention to support long-term development and investment in the faculty hired for the program.

Needless to say, there is one major problem which often hampers fast-track development. Many of the faculty in these circumstances may receive split-appointments and or split academic responsibilities which come with a requirement to teach at least two other classes in the area of training (e.g., linguistics, literature, etc.). The faculty member often struggles with these dual responsibilities, facing the challenge of maintaining an acceptable academic standing as well as sustaining a reputable and successful language program. Not many faculty members are able or willing to subject themselves to such pressures, and often the language program ends up being a low priority and development is either minimal or negligible. Some language programs have found a way around these obstacles by first seeking a clear understanding with the unit head and the unit faculty to ensure unwavering support for the language program's activities. The program may select activities which reflect the needs of the administering unit or the institution at large. For example, where culture is an important institutional interest (multiculturalism), the language program may emphasize that by tailoring the language class to fit the students' multicultural requirements in their degree programs. Emphasis on the structural patterns of the language or learning the language for research purposes should be secondary while the need to know and understand other peoples of the world and their cultures takes a primary focus in the class.

3.5 Perspective for Development

The strength of the linkage between a language program, the unit head, other units, and the institution at large will define prevailing and future perspectives of the language program. Programs with a strong foundation will do well in this relationship. Development plans for an African language program should begin at the home department where the relationship between the unit head and the language program is welcome and strong. A strong relationship at this level will establish a foundation that cannot be destroyed easily, even if the faculty, instructor, or teaching assistant positions are changed periodically. It is likely that the unit head will seek a strong replacement to ensure continuity of the traditions in place as well as to preserve the program's reputation and the reputation it brings to the unit and the institution at large.

Issues of quality and evaluation are also very important in

this perspective for development. Quality and evaluation can only be met if the need to develop the field of African languages is taken seriously. Issues of who should be teaching African languages as well as how it should be taught must be major concerns for the program as well as the head of the unit. Undoubtedly, to ensure effectiveness, the most desirable of programming and instruction is one that combines the three types (A-C) described earlier. Having a faculty member in charge of programming (designing and teaching) will ensure stability and consistency in the types of teaching materials acquired and used in the classrooms. Most African language programs suffer from inconsistencies in teaching materials, methodologies, and teaching styles. In many cases, each teacher walks in and out of a program with their own materials, agenda, objectives, and goals. This is a critical problem considering that over 60% of African language instructors and teaching assistants have limited tenure (between one and two years).

The evaluation of African language programs is problematic at present due to the fact that each institution is independent and is not governed by a central body and an agreed curriculum. An organization like the African Language Teachers Association (ALTA) can serve as the central body. However, it is unclear how an organization like ALTA which is, without doubt, passionate on consistency and standards, can mandate an evaluation procedure without seeming intrusive against these programs. The best ALTA can do is to play a linking role rather than a policing role. Such a role will be less imposing and more protective of the programs that are struggling to survive institutionally. A linking role can be played through hosting workshops, visiting programs, and looking for ways to involve such programs in summer institutes.

This means that an effort has to be made to provide programming support to bring these programs to the desired level and
offer incentives for good programming before a meaningful
evaluation can be initiated. Such success is only possible if there
is a stronger link between the Title VI programs (which have
guaranteed resources), and non-Title VI programs (which have
restricted resources). Together they can embark on a national
development strategy. In a small way, this can be done by ALTA
which has already put in place development plans through its
task forces whose responsibility includes monitoring as well as
initiating field wide projects. For example, the Swahili task force
has developed a teacher's manual which outlines teaching
strategies. What is needed to complement the manual is a student's
manual which will outline strategies for learning. In addition,
they have a number of technology related projects including the
development of instructional video materials. The Yoruba and
Hausa task forces have initiated technology activities and have
begun to identify existing resources for a major field development
plan. Two new task forces (the West African Languages Task
Force and the South African Languages Task Force) are in their
formative stages and will, undoubtedly, move in the same
development directions as the task forces of Swahili, Yoruba,
and Hausa.

4. COLLABORATIVE EFFORTS

Collaborative initiatives will enhance field-wide development.
Until 1992, there were two camps, the Title VI and non-Title VI
programs, under which African language programming could be
found. Not much had been done to foster a strong linkage between

the two camps even though the non-Title VI programs played a significant role in sustaining Title VI programs by providing students at the graduate level.

The history of the rift between non-Title VI and Title VI programs, despite this major role played by non-Title VI programs, lies in the way African language programs were established at most Title VI centers, namely under the auspices of African Studies programs. The programming format, strategy, focus, and objectives followed the same patterns as found in commonly taught languages. The sole purpose for the instruction of language was to equip graduate students with language skills to enable them to do research in and about Africa. This is still the tradition even though the clientele (students who take a language) has changed. Despite the fact that those programs are now flooded by undergraduate students (and in fact have been sustained by undergraduate enrollments), language programs at Title VI centers have not made a conscious effort to evaluate this change and to lay down new strategies to meet the needs of the new clients. Non-Title VI African language programs, on the other hand, did not have the same goals and objectives. Consequently, their clientele has consistently remained undergraduate students with varying objectives for taking an African language class.

Programs that have recognized this fact have adjusted accordingly to meet the needs of these students and as a result are running very successful programs which compete with the more advanced LCTLs like Japanese and Chinese. In addition to aiding those students who need to fulfill a language requirement, the main objective for many non-Title VI programs is not to prepare students for research in Africa; rather, it is to introduce a non Indo-European language, to cultivate students' interests in a broader view of the world. The hope is often that such an introduction will persuade a student to learn more about the culture (through anthropology), to learn the geography and history of the continent, and to attempt to understand the political and economic ideologies found on the continent.

Program heads are aware that such an introduction at the early stages of the students' educations may lead to a much stronger preparation for research or work in Africa. As such, program heads do not, in a subtle way, make students feel that interest in Africa is a prerequisite to enrolling or doing well in the class. Providing the knowledge is the central theme. Consequential results are welcome if they lead to a keener interest in African studies. Experience shows that a program with broad goals, goals that are less expansive, attract students from a variety of cultural backgrounds and academic interests. Therefore, what we need to focus on as we discuss development in African language programming for the twenty-first century are the goals and objectives that reflect present and future trends. We need to establish a rationale for teaching a particular language, for developing specific teaching strategies, for adopting certain specific technologies and, most of all, for preparing students to be lifelong learners.

A national perspective must be inclusive and must be able to assess the productivity of individual programs and the link between the existing constituencies. ALTA can be a strong link, one that can provide for 90% of the language programs that are not fully represented in the Association of African Studies Programs (AASP, which is largely a consortium of Title VI programs). ALTA can serve not only as a link between all language programs and AASP but also as an instrument of change in the way non-Title VI programs are viewed and supported in various institutions. There is a need for ALTA to expand its task forces beyond the three commonly taught African languages (Swahili,

Yoruba, Hausa). A national agenda must include ways in which the number of African languages taught nationally is increased and most of all, professionalized. The increase should pay attention to representation and deal with at least two languages from the four main regions (northern, eastern, southern, and western Africa). Focus should first be on Group I languages which are more frequently taught on college campuses in the United States. Subsequent attention should be given to languages in Groups II and III with a wider adoption of tutorial formats and distance learning formats at the intermediate and advanced levels. Teaching with technology should be encouraged and developed for all levels of instruction. The goal in the development plan should be efficiency at the instructional level and cost-effectiveness.

The newly instituted National African Languages Resource Center (NALRC) at the University of Wisconsin is a fresh and welcome addition to these efforts. The Center's goals and objectives are: to provide resources and training that enhance the teaching and learning of African languages; to establish and maintain networks of African language teachers, professional language teacher associations, and other foreign language centers; to coordinate African language teaching and learning resources available in the United States; to disseminate information and materials on the teaching and learning of African languages; and to evaluate and promote African language instructional programs. It will definitely transform the field.

5. TEACHING MATERIALS DEVELOPMENT

Developing teaching materials and other teaching resources remains the biggest challenge for African languages. African languages do not have enough textbooks audio/video materials for instructional purposes. Consequently, teachers and students have very little to choose from. African language teachers should consider this a serious problem which requires immediate resolution. Although textbooks are not usually used productively in the teaching of languages, their role is quite obvious, namely to serve as a tool that complements the teacher's instructional role and enhances the student's learning efforts. As such, the textual material should provide cultural information which is comprehensive enough to provide the student with a good foundation for further study or research on the language and its culture. Of the available textbooks, not many include a cultural component. A cultural curriculum for the learning of an African language must include (both in the teaching mode and in the textbooks) a cultural component which consists of cultural notes and exercises that enable the student to retain cultural knowledge and information. It should also encourage the student to explore and appreciate aspects of the target culture that help him or her to understand and appreciate his or her own culture. Before we provide our recommendations, let's examine the current condition of available materials.

5.1 Available Textbooks

In a study of eighteen textbooks for the teaching of African languages (Dwyer, Moshi, Schleicher 1999) five categories were identified.

TEXTLESS TEXTBOOKS These textbooks can be characterized as grammar-translation based. They are intended to provide enough information to engage the student in accurate translation exercises from the target language to their L1 or other languages. There is no evidence, in some of the textbooks, of the need for the student to be informed of the phonological, morphological, or syntactic structure of the language. That knowledge is assumed since the main aim is to provide the student with only those skills that are deemed necessary for accurate translation of written texts and not necessarily oral skills. To provide additional help to the student, some textbooks offer translation samples that serve as a guide. Because of their orientation, the text materials do not have a coherent theme and are not presented in any particular sequence.

To some extent, these texts reflect the position of many language programs, one that was borrowed from the tradition in Indo-European commonly taught languages (German, French, Spanish), a tradition that is mandated by institutions of higher education as they prepare students to fulfill a language requirement, particularly for students of language, linguistics, and literatures.

AUDIO-LINGUAL TEXTS Compared with textless textbooks described above, audio-lingual texts are not very different in their thematic and presentational structure. They are basically textbooks with grammar-driven monologues and dialogues. Typically, these books present dialogues which do not demonstrate an awareness of a need to portray sensitivity to the special cultural contexts of the targeted community.

Like the textless textbooks, the rationale for the development of audio-lingual texts is clearly to prepare the students for a specific goal: to read, understand, and accurately translate texts. Knowledge of the culture and other social aspects of speakers of the target language appears to have been treated as secondary and often remains unexplored. It seems that the emphasis was to maintain a strict academic approach to language learning, an attempt to preserve the credibility of learning a less commonly taught language by making *learning of the language* and the *learning about the language* indistinguishable. While this was well received at the time these text were developed, the change in African language clientele (from mainly graduate students to predominately undergraduate students) has forced language teachers to rethink the effectiveness of these textbooks in today's classroom. In fact, it appears that these textbooks (and the teaching methodology adopted as a consequence of it) may have contributed to the reluctance shown by college administrators to readily make resources available for LCTLs.

ADVANCED AUDIO-LINGUAL TEXTS The distinction between an audio-lingual and advanced audio-lingual text lies in the latter's having accompanying audio tapes which are intended to reinforce the text materials. Students are encouraged to listen to the tapes and are asked occasionally to repeat words and phrases. Students are encouraged to repeat the audio text and record it for playback. The goal is to allow the student to evaluate his or her input comparing the pre-recordings with their own reproductions while they make adjustments as needed to perfect their speech. It is also a subtle memory training technique.

There is another distinction. Although grammar, morphology, and phonology are also emphasized in these texts, they are not totally grammar driven. They show an awareness of the need to present cultural information in the lesson schema by selecting cultural themes for each lesson (greetings, marketing, visiting, directions to places, etc.) which are culturally situated. Dialogues (not monologues) are favored, and notes that explain the cultural dimensions of a text are especially beyond the context at hand. There may also be some additional BTW (By-the-Way) cultural notes (that is, cultural notes that are not directly connected to the theme of the lesson). There are ample illustrations that are sometimes used to enhance the cultural presentation. The study also notes that textbooks intended for second or third year of instruction are likely to be completely thematically based.

CULTURE-ORIENTED TEXTS These textbooks incorporate a fair amount of cultural material and cultural notes (although they could do more). They orient each lesson toward the presentation of a cultural theme and tend to include dialogues and monologues from the very beginning. Cultural topics include the family, community, main occupations, health, recreation, and aesthetics. Grammar sequencing is still important but it is often designed to accommodate the cultural design. In some cases, each section has explanatory notes and exercises intended to draw out the most significant cultural points.

INTERCULTURAL PERSPECTIVE TEXTS This category represents many of the textbooks written since 1979. For the most part, they try to make culture an integral part of the knowledge to be acquired; however, intercultural sensitivity does not receive much attention. Instead of emphasizing cultural differences, equal emphasis is put on similarities and differences. Thus, lessons contain explanatory cultural notes and cultural and intercultural queries. An attempt is made to include a large display of photographs and/or hand drawn pictures that are overtly as well as covertly associated with the main theme of the lesson.

5.2 Video- and Computer-Assisted Teaching Materials

Until recently, no films or video suitable in language classes were available. Films, most of which are in English, were intended to portray the speakers of the target language as primitive. While they may serve a specific purpose such as describing the history, anthropology, or the political economy of the people, they tend to provide negative cultural feedback to the learner.

Recently, there has been a surge in the development of video and computer teaching materials that are authentic and culturally rich. The leading language is Swahili with a variety of videos in Swahili, English, or both with subtitles. Many of them were developed at the University of Georgia, and a few by other commercial and religious media production companies. There is also a CD-ROM developed by John Mugane at Stanford University (Mugane 1998) which makes use of selected video materials produced at the University of Georgia (Moshi 1990, 1996, 1998). In the area of computer-assisted teaching materials, there are a Hypercard computer-assisted materials project at Michigan State University and an internet based material development at the University of Pennsylvania and Stanford University. Specialists in Hausa and Yoruba have also embarked on the creation of video-and computer-assisted teaching materials. Specialists in Hausa have completed a set of videos intended for advanced Hausa instruction and are now developing a companion CD-ROM. A computer-assisted program using HyperCard has also been in progress for a number of years at UCLA. It is now being tested at a limited number of language programs across the nation. Yoruba specialists have completed two CD-ROMs (Schleicher 1997, 1999) with companion textbooks which are popularly used at many institutions at the elementary (*Jé K' A So Yorubá* Schleicher 1993) and intermediate (*Jé K' A Ka Yorubá* Schleicher 1999) levels. It is more than likely that other languages, especially the Group I languages, will follow the example of these three languages in both materials development and general field development. As we can see, there is very little to go around and there are not enough resources available from which teachers and students can choose. Needless to say, the new video-and computer-assisted teaching materials provide more information on culture than the textbooks, especially the first two text materials identified in the study mentioned here.

6. IMPLICATIONS FOR DEVELOPMENT

As noted earlier and as the discussion in section five shows, the development of the field of African languages is critical. It is also true to say that the field has come a long way considering that development did not start until 1990 when the African Language Teachers Association (ALTA) embarked on the task of shaping the future of the field. Although we are still behind the major languages (e.g., German, French, Spanish) and some of the less commonly taught languages (like Arabic, Japanese, Chinese, and Southeast Asian languages), we are making steady progress which will finally put African language programming on the national map and on the fast track for development in the twenty-first century. Based on the progress of textbooks, videos, and computer-assisted materials, there appears to be a clear pattern of development, one that will lead the African language programs to a stage that reflects new trends in foreign language instruction in the United States.

CHAPTER TWO

The State of African Language Instruction in the U.S.

An Inventory of Programs, Assets, and Resources

1. INTRODUCTION

African language study, as a university subject in the United States, began in the 1960s, mainly as part of a general U.S. foreign policy initiative to expand knowledge of previously untaught or less commonly taught languages. With the exception of the University of Wisconsin-Madison (the only university with a department of African languages and literatures), U.S. universities have not until recently viewed the study of African languages as a field in its own right, although language fields such as Latin, French, Spanish, Russian, Chinese, or Japanese have long since enjoyed that sort of legitimacy. Even at the University of Wisconsin, the Department of African Languages and Literature does not include bachelors, masters, or doctoral degree programs in any of the African languages taught there (Hausa, Swahili, or Yoruba). Instead, the Department offers a B.A., M.A., or Ph.D. in African languages and Literature with a requirement of two or three years of study of African language. Other courses which count towards the degree in African Languages and Literatures are African literature or African linguistics courses taught in English. In most cases, students are not encouraged to write their M.A. theses or Ph.D. dissertations on the literature or linguistics of the African languages they have spent three years learning.

The dilemma faced here is in the answer to the critical question many programs ask: How much of a language does a student have to learn in two or three years to qualify him or her for a degree in that language? The answer is that they cannot learn enough language in such a short period. In a department such as Wisconsin's Department of African Languages and Literatures where students are not encouraged to set a goal of achieving a degree in any African language, their two or three years of study will only serve to fulfil their language requirement because their degree is in general African languages and literatures which requires a demonstration of a specific level of language proficiency.

A dilemma faced by Wisconsin's department has its roots in the following three principal types of African language programs across the nation: (1) those associated with African-American studies where one or two African languages are taught to enhance a set of core courses (e.g., history and literature) focused on

Africa and the Diaspora; (2) those associated with departments of linguistics, comparative literatures, or joint linguistics and modern languages, where two or three African languages are offered as full courses and other least commonly taught African languages are made available on demand. Their main goal is to prepare graduate students for field research while attracting undergraduates who fancy an African language for their language requirement. These programs have the advantage of a small core of linguists and a large group of teaching assistants; (3) those associated with African Studies programs where a much wider range of languages can be offered on a regular basis.

As described in chapter one, African Studies programs and centers have the advantage of federal funding which can be used to maintain or expand language offerings in addition to developing area studies through interdisciplinary course offerings. The federal funding which is obtained through tri-annual competitions are the lifeline of African Studies which explains the efforts made in maintaining a critical mass of African languages—a major factor for favorable federal funding consideration.

Needless to say, and as noted in chapter one, the status of African languages, at the institutional level when entrenched in either of the three types discussed above, cannot be better than low or average. They have neither autonomy nor power to set goals that can lead to the establishment of a degree program even in clear cases like that of the Department of African Languages and Literatures at Wisconsin.

The dilemma has also forced specialists in African languages to pursue career goals in different disciplines such as linguistics, anthropology, comparative literatures, language education, and African studies. Consequently, the field has suffered from a lack of dedicated expertise for many years. The birth of ALTA in

1988 has served as a means to cultivate a field expertise base which has assumed the responsibility of reseeding the African language programs across the nation.

In this chapter, we will focus on a study whose goal was to provide a review of the African language programs in the United States.

2. SCOPE

This study is not intended to be a systematic review of every African language program in the U.S., nor is it one person's view of where the African language profession stands. Rather, it is a databased study which attempts to obtain an overall picture of African language instruction today as carried out by African language teachers in the U.S. The report deals with African language educational practice rather than with educational theory or research. Most of the data presented below comes from two survey questionnaires collected from 23 African language programs.

3. QUESTIONNAIRE DEVELOPMENT

So that the questionnaire would reflect more than one person's point of view, several of the most important periodicals in foreign language education were perused for the purpose of identifying topics to be included. Opinions of other language professionals in African languages and other foreign languages were sought before developing the questionnaire. The final draft was authenticated by the authors with additional help from members of the ALTA Executive Board.

The intention was to explore five major areas of African language instruction. Our awareness of the changing demographics in African language instruction over the past decade mitigated our desire to locate the African languages clientele and types (whether undergraduate or graduate students) as well as their motivations.

The second major area concerned characteristics of African language teaching personnel. There is much talk in the field about the problem of hiring full-time language instructors to teach African languages in most programs, about a lack of thorough teacher training programs for African language faculty members and teaching assistants, and about the effects that untrained language instructors have on the quality of instruction. In order to gather information about the African language teaching profession with respect to these areas of concern, we wanted to find out the following from our respondents—those who coordinate the African language programs: (a) what percentage of their appointments are allocated to program coordination; (b) what percentage of the instructors appointments are allocated to teaching African languages; (c) what the minimal qualifications for teaching assistants are—language proficiency, field of specialization, and degree of language teaching training.

Our third major area of concern was the number of African languages taught on a regular basis during the regular academic sessions and/or during the summer sessions. We were cognizant of the fact that there are between 1,000 and 1,500 languages spoken in Africa (see Dwyer and Moshi 1994) and that no program could possibly offer all of them. All we wanted to know was what African languages had been taught over the past five academic years and during summer in the schools we had targeted for the survey. We were also interested in the levels (elementary, intermediate, advanced) available to students and whether there are specific degree programs in any of the African languages offered at the institution.

Our fourth area of concern was of current teaching practices and curriculum content in African language courses at all levels. In the recent past, journals in foreign language education have contained many articles on the topics of communicative competence, career education, the teaching of foreign culture, individualized instruction, use of authentic materials, and the use of the target language in language instruction. We were, therefore, interested in finding out whether our field's practitioners were implementing ideas presented in the professional literature in their own language instruction. Of interest also was whether there are Africa-focused courses that use African languages as their medium of instruction.

Because of the attention paid to the testing of foreign language skills, we were also interested in gaining insights into the practices by African language teachers in testing their students' listening comprehension and communicative competence. We wanted to know if they were testing discrete vocabulary items or using dictation as a testing device.

Included in the questionnaire were questions which allowed the respondents to give generalized information about their experiences, their visions, field problems, and other language-teaching and-learning related issues. In the following section, we will present the findings and discussions.

4. DATA FINDINGS AND DISCUSSIONS

4.1 The Changing Demographics of African Language Instruction

As noted in chapter one, and also by Bennett (1985), the structure of African language programs in the 1960s was generally administered through linguistics departments using a linguist/informant model of instruction with scanty and non-standardized materials. In addition, the targeted were graduate students aiming to do funded research in Africa. But by the early 1970s, there was a sharp rise in undergraduate enrollments in African languages (especially Swahili). This rise was associated with the Black Power Movement and the simultaneous decline in levels of government funding for graduate programs in African languages.

Table 2.1 shows the percentage of undergraduate and graduate students that currently study African languages. On the average, about 70.5% of those who study African languages are undergraduates, while about 29.5% are graduate students. This correlates with the observation by Arasanyin, et al. (1996) that about 35.9% of those who study African languages do so for research purposes. Comparing these two surveys, it seems that the majority of those who study African languages for research preparation are graduate students. Interestingly, graduate students constitute a minority of African language learners. The low percentage of graduate students who study African languages (compared with undergraduates) supports our assumption that their main motivation is preparation for field research. Observe the findings outlined in Table 2.1 below.

%	1	2	3	4	5	6	7	8	9	10	11	12	13	14	15	Avg.
Graduate	40	10	50	10	40	10	50	50	10	10	15	10	10	15	25	23.6
Under-graduate	60	90	50	90	60	90	50	50	90	90	85	90	90	85	75	76.4

Table 2.1. Percentage of graduate and undergraduate students in African languages.

An obvious question related to these figures in Table 2.1 is why do students study African languages. Schuh (1988) notes that interest in African or Third World cultures or area studies was the number one reason why students chose to learn African languages; field research was number two. Arasanyin, et al. (1996), shows, that 69.6% of learners indicated heritage, family demands, insights into ethnic culture, or access to a non-European body of knowledge as their main motivations for learning African languages. More than 42% of those who enrolled in African language courses did so to fulfil an institutional curriculum requirement. Only 35.9% claimed to be studying African langua-ges to prepare for research in Africa or about African topics. Both Schuh (1988) and Arasanyin, et al. (1996) conclude that, compared to the 1960s, research and the fulfillment of fellowship-related language requirements are no longer the major reasons for students to learn African languages. These conclusions are borne-out in this study as shown in Table 2.1. Our conclusion is that undergraduate students have never taken African languages for reasons related to research-or fellowship-related language requirements reasons and it is not surprising that more undergraduate than graduate students take African languages today.

4.2 Professional Background

We asked our respondents several questions about their professional backgrounds: (1) Who were your African language faculty and what percentage of their appointments were allocated to the teaching of African languages? (2) Who were your language coordinators and what percentage of their time was allocated to the coordination of your program? (3) Were there teaching assistants? (4) What were the minimal teaching qualifications and proficiency levels expected? (5) What were the major fields of specialization for the teachers? (6) Did the teachers receive teacher training prior to assuming their teaching responsibilities (if so, to what extent)?

Table 2.2 shows that of 34 African language faculty, only 12 actually devote 100% of their time to African language teaching. If we compare to the early 1980s, when about 35% of the faculty actually taught an African language, 100% is a great improvement. Schuh (1988) notes that there are three types of African classroom staffing situations: language courses taught by faculty members only; those taught by teaching assistants only; and those taught by faculty and a native speaker. He adds that the first two modes are appropriate if the faculty and teaching assistants are not only fluent in the language but are also trained in language pedagogy. He, has a big problem however, with the third mode (the faculty member and a native speaker) which he claims:

> . . . harkens back to the "linguist and informant" mode of the 1940s and 1950s, where the "naive informant" was the preferred model for students. Not only has enlightened language pedagogy long recognized the shortcomings of the mimicry and the drill method of teaching which is attendant to this teaching mode, it is degrading to the informant, who is little more than a language production machine.

Even though Schuh's survey shows that some African language programs still practice the faculty-and-native-speaker mode, this practice is rapidly disappearing in most programs.

Univ.	1	2	3	4	5	6	7	8	9	10	11	12	13	14	15
0 %	•	•		•		•	•				•	•	•	•	
25 %	•														
33 %	••	••													
50 %	••		•			••		••		•	•				
75 %						•									
100 %			•••	•	•	•	•••		••						•

Table 2.2. Percentage of African language faculty member's appointment allocated to the teaching of African languages.

Bennett (1985) attributed the increase in the faculty/lecturer only or the teaching assistant only modes to the following three trends: (1) the number of Africans who enroll in American degree programs is growing, providing a larger pool of Africans with appropriate academic qualifications; (2) the effect of affirmative action principles, giving preference to qualified blacks if available; (3) and the fact that an African is somewhat more likely to be interested in teaching his or her language than an American trained in theory but without the skills of a native speaker.

In spite of this improvement in the staffing of many African language courses—as shown in Bennett (1985), Schuh (1988), and this survey—what is still disturbing is the number of faculty with expertise in the teaching of African languages who do not spend any time teaching African languages but who instead teach other courses that serve their primary scholarly interests such as linguistics, anthropology, literature, etc. Needless to say, many of those who spend 100% of their time teaching African language do so because of an inability to secure teaching positions in their primary areas of interest. As such, teaching African languages is, to them, a stop-gap measure while they wait for opportunities that suit their interests better.

As noted earlier, this has much to do with whether such teachers find the teaching of African languages professionally credible in the academy. Do they hold the same credibility as French teachers? Are they able to deal with disturbing inquisitions from colleagues which include questions like "What do you do apart from teaching Hausa, Swahili, or Yoruba?" Such questions suggest that teaching an African language cannot be considered credible. Young professionals in African language pedagogy still struggle with these perceptions from the academy. These perceptions force them to devote more of their time to research and publication in other disciplines which hold more prestige in the academy. There is, therefore, a constant struggle between a desired balance in their research in language teaching and the more prestigious discipline (e.g., linguistics or literature). It is disconcerting to note that while a French or Spanish assistant professor can get tenure doing research on French or Spanish pedagogy, it is still very difficult for an African language assistant professor to get tenure with research on only African language pedagogy. The requirement is that they show a balance between pedagogy and (African) linguistics or literature.

This, we contend, is an undue burden that few would like to take except when it is the only option for survival in the academy. This also lends support to what we mentioned earlier; the dilemma facing the field of African languages development is a consequence of a weakened field expertise base. There is, therefore, a need to begin encouraging professional African language teachers by rewarding young faculty members whose strengths are in African language pedagogy research and teaching. The perception that the African language pedagogists are individuals who have not been successful in their research in African linguistics or literature only discourages them and further weakens the expertise base. The expertise base should not be populated by non-professionals or individuals whose scholarly interests lie elsewhere. Luckily, ALTA, as the active voice of authority, has began to change that perception. The quality of papers now published on African language pedagogy (JALTA 1999, 2000) reflect this achievement.

Univ.	1	2	3	4	5	6	7	8	9	10	11	12	13	14	15
0 %		•				•	•		•	•	•	•		•	•
10 %			•												
25 %				•										•	
50 %	•				•			::					•		

Table 2.3. Percentage of coordinators' time allocated to coordinating African language classes.

Table 2.3 shows the percentage of coordinators' time devoted to coordinating language classes. Clearly the majority of coordinators spend little or no time in the business that affects the language program the most: coordinating the language classes. Thus, they do not contribute as much as possible to the expertise base. Their limited role can also be explain the low status accorded to teachers entrusted with the task of making the program sustainable.

Table 2.3 also suggests something else which is crucial in understanding the status quo. The category "language coordinator" in African language programs is understood differently compared with what it means in other foreign language programs. Their roles are clearly marked in Dwyer and Moshi (1994, 4) who define an African language coordinator as the person responsible for:

(1) maintaining an overall view of the operation of the program, (2) cooperating with and maintaining communication with other Title VI African language coordinators, and (3) initiating activities which will improve the learning of African languages both nationally and locally.

While coordinators in many European language departments, are fluent in the languages they coordinate, it is not so in African language departments. Most coordinators work with TAs or native speakers who teach these languages. Thus, the role of the coordinator is either advisory or purely administrative. We concur with Dwyer and Moshi that, "many of the idiosyncratic properties of an African language program can be traced to the degree of involvement the Language Coordinator is expected to have, and can have, with the African language program."

On the required levels of language proficiency for TAs (or instructors), the survey focused on expectations recruiting institutions. This was crucial (based on Table 2.2), for we showed that only a few of the African language faculty devote 100% of their time to teaching African languages. Our respondents were asked specifically what level of language proficiency was required for their TAs or instructors available, the next favored choice was a teacher with an Advanced or Advanced Plus level of proficiency. When asked about the respondents preferred in fields of specialization and teaching experience or the teaching assistants or instructors, more than 70% did not show a preference either way. The remaining 30% preferred teachers specializing in linguistics.

The implication is that the pool of instructors may include graduate students from disciplines other than those closely linked to language and linguistics: law, engineering, agriculture, history, political science, etc. The minimum qualification would be native-speaker skills in the language. The question here is *Does being a competent speaker of a language in and of itself qualify anyone as an excellent teacher of the language?* Proper and adequate training in language pedagogy and explicit knowledge about the language and its culture are critical, certainly more important (more important than being a native speaker of the language). Speaking the language is simply not enough of a credential for an institution to entrust an instructor with teaching naive learners of a foreign language and culture. This is clearly what Schuh had in mind as he notes, "It is nothing short of being irresponsible to appoint someone as a 'Teaching Assistant' who has no other qualifications than being a native speaker of the language to be taught" (1988, 7).

About 60% said that their TAs or instructors do not have any special language training while about 40% claimed that they give their TAs "some kind of training or workshop." The degree of training was minimal a: one day workshop or weekend long training. Needless to say, this is not unique to the field of African languages. Speaking of Chinese, Walton (1989) makes the observation that in Chinese there is no teacher training and that what is evident is that teachers adapt to idiosyncratic institutional settings. He also notes that in the case of LCTLs: "some programs, desperate for LCTL teachers, hire instructors without going through the normal certification procedures or checks on professional competence." Walton's concern for Chinese seems to echo the current situation in African language pedagogy. For "truly foreign" languages (Jorden and Walton 1997) such as African languages, one would expect that these languages will be taught by TAs who are well trained to teach both the "fact" and the "act" of the language.

There is no question that the lack of credible teacher training programs for African languages has quite obvious consequences in terms of learner outcomes. It has not helped our student enrollment and retention either. Good students do not hang around when there are weaknesses in instruction. The field intends to make a Language Teaching Methods course a prerequisite for future teaching assistants as an attempt to solve some of the problems associated with the lack of a formalized TA training, both at the institutional and national levels. We need to caution also that, simply attending a method's course in and of itself does not automatically or necessarily make anyone a "master teacher." All it will do is enlighten the prospective teacher by acquainting him or her with the *what, how,* and *why* of a language class.

While the majority of the field expertise base has done very well in African language pedagogy, for the most part this success

41

has been won through trial and error. Although one could make the excuse that development has lagged behind because we did not have ALTA and, therefore, lacked the incentive to develop a professional African language field, that excuse will only be valid if we show different results in the next few years. ALTA, as strong as it is growing, is a statement of our commitment to this field. The next best step would be the development of a good, solid, and reliable TA training program, a way to keep good students in our language programs and to encourage professionals to add to the expertise base.

4.3 African Language Offerings

As opposed to a single-language field such as Japanese, Chinese, or Russian, the field of African language pedagogy in the United States consists of a multiplicity of subfields of varying capacities and resources. This is a direct response to the linguistic diversity of Africa (with as many as 1000 languages). In order to deal with this diversity, and using such criteria as numbers of speakers, official status, material development and other resources, ATLA has identified 82 African languages as priority languages which merit serious attention in the U.S. educational system.

For practical reasons, it is still not possible for any one institution to offer all 82 languages identified as priorities. We, therefore, wanted to know, from the survey, which of those languages are frequently offered during the academic year and summer programs. We also wanted to know if any of the African language programs have degree programs in any of these languages. Table 2.4 summarizes our findings, showing languages that have been taught on a regular basis at least twice during the past five years. (This survey excludes Arabic, which is housed outside of African language programs at most universities. In addition, Arabic teachers do not hold membership in ALTA nor do they consider themselves part of the African languages expertise base.)

Univ.	1	2	3	4	5	6	7	8	9	10	11	12	13	14	15
Swahili 1	•	•	•	•	•	•	•	•	•	•	•	•	•	•	•
Swahili 2	•	•	•	•	•	•	•	•	•	•	•	•	•	•	•
Swahili 3	•	•	•	•	•	•	•			•				•	•
Hausa 1	•			•		•	•	•	•						
Hausa 2	•			•		•	•	•	•						
Hausa 3	•					•	•								
Yoruba 1		•	•		•	•				•		•	•		•
Yoruba 2		•	•		•	•				•		•	•		•
Yoruba 3			•			•									
Bambara 1	•			•			•							•	
Bambara 2	•			•										•	
Bambara 3															
Zulu 1			•			•	•							•	
Zulu 2			•			•	•							•	
Shona 1	•	•				•									
Shona 2	•	•				•									
Shona 3	•					•									
Mandinka 1					•										
Mandinka 2					•										
Chichewa 1			•												
Chichewa 2			•												
Fulfulde 1	•														
Fulfulde 2	•														
Fulfulde 3	•														
Lingala 1														•	
Lingala 2														•	
Wolof 1														•	
Wolof 2														•	
Amharic 1	•														
Amharic 2	•														
Amharic 3	•														
Akan 1		•													
Akan 2		•													

Table 2.4. Programs that have taught African languages regularly (at least twice over five years).

Not included in this list are a number of languages which were described by respondents as taught "on demand." We decided not to include them in the data because "on demand" (i.e., subject to availability of students who request this language) does not necessarily show how often these courses are taught. An examination of the data shows that very few universities in the U.S. teach more than three or four languages, and a total of thirteen languages are taught regularly. This is an increase in the number of African language offerings when we compare the results to Schuh's (1988) findings.

"On demand" languages, were taught between the 1940s and the 1960s using the linguist-informant model or faculty native speaker model. The linguist was the faculty person who team taught the class with a native speaker who served as an informant. The faculty, in most cases, did not possess any proficiency in the language, but had linguistic knowledge of the structure. The native speaker conducted drills with the students, something Schuh (1988) takes issue with (see earlier discussion regarding this model). This model fell out of favor by the 1970s; however, we assert that the African language coordinator structure formed in the late 1980s, appears to have replaced the 1940s-1960s model. There is no language proficiency requirement for coordinators, particularly those who coordinate "on demand" languages (in some cases between 4-6 languages at one time). It is disconcerting because the standards would not be tolerated in languages such as French, Spanish, Russian, or Japanese for which language coordinators are required to possess acceptable language proficiencies in order to supervise teaching assistants. The unfortunate part, too, is that many of these language coordinators are not trained pedagogists, yet they are given the responsibility of training teaching assistants whose only strength is that they are native speakers of the language they are asked to teach. A coordinator should be equipped to provide leadership, make decisions on textbook selections, curriculum development, lesson plans, and assessment of outcomes.

This should not be different in the field of African languages. The mere fact that the African language coordinator coordinates the teaching of many languages that he or she does not speak makes his or her job a very challenging one. The coordinator should be prepared to deal with teachers' morale. In many cases teachers of "on demand" languages have just one or two students which means that hourly compensation is very low, providing little incentive to be committed to teaching. It is naive of the institutions to think that they can cultivate loyalty from such teachers when they pay them less than what they can make by flipping hamburgers at fast-food restaurants.

There are additional questions to address concerning "on demand" courses (which many institutions include in their listings as courses offered on a regular basis):

- How much of the language does the student learn in this mode?
- Should these languages be advertised at all as languages that we teach?
- From experience, most of the students come out of "on demand" courses knowing a few structures of the language. If this is the case, shouldn't we list these courses as linguistics ("Structure of an African Language") instead of as language courses?

There are definitely some advantages to offering "on demand" courses. Bennett (1985, 8) claims that "given a competent and energetic coordinator and careful choice of native speakers as instructors, the coordinator/native speaker model can work well for 'on demand' languages." This model can provide a wide selection of languages expanding the scope of a language program operating on a rather small budget.

The problem, however, is that we may be misguided by cost effectiveness aspects of a program and compromise pedagogical effectiveness. At worst, it raises the probability of ineffective teaching and false claims in program advertising, since it is not always the case that an appropriate instructor for a given language is readily available. It also presents African language programs simply as a services of an institution, catering to graduate students with foreign language fellowships.

As Schuh (1988, 9) succinctly puts it, "No one would expect a Spanish department to agree to teach Catalan or a German department to teach Frisian just because a student or two said they 'needed' to study one of those languages." Why should instructors in African languages be expected to teach any of Africa's 1000 languages "on demand." Or why should we claim that we can do so? The field of African language pedagogy will be better off if we focus our efforts on the languages where demand is greatest and where there is the most competence among language teachers.

Table 2.5 shows African languages that have been offered during the summer for the past five years.

Univ.	1	2	3	4	5	6	7	8	9	10	11	12	13	14	15
Swahili 1	•		•			•	•								
Swahili 2	•		•			•	•								
Swahili 3	•		•			•	•								
Hausa 1						•									
Hausa 2							•								
Hausa 3							•								
Yoruba 1		•	•		•										
Yoruba 2		•	•												
Bambara 1				•											
Bambara 2				•											
Zulu 1			•												
Zulu 2			•												
Zulu 3							•								
Shona 1	•														
Shona 2	•														
Shona 3	•														
Mandinka 1					•										
Chichewa 1			•												
Lingala 2														•	
Wolof 2														•	
Amharic 1	•														•
Amharic 2	•														
Amharic 3	•														
Akan 1		•													
Akan 2		•													
Setswana 1									•						

Table 2.5 African languages not offered during summer for at least two years.

The number of languages taught during the summer seems to be more than those taught during the regular academic years. The reason for this is because these summer language programs are mostly supported by their home institution's funds or by Foreign Language and Area Studies Fellowships (FLAS).

In response to the question whether or not there is a degree program in any particular African language offered at the respondents' institutions, all respondents indicated that, as of now, there is no degree program in any of the African languages that they teach. What this implies is that the majority of the students who study African languages are not necessarily required to study the language beyond three or four semesters. This also explains why most programs are usually left with about three or four students at the advanced level. Most students leave the program after their third or fourth semester of language studies, except for a few students who choose to continue for personal reasons.

4.4 Current Teaching Practices

There has been much discussion in foreign language education literature over the past several years about the concept of *communicative competence* in a foreign language learning environment. One of the main themes in second-language acquisition research today is how important it is for the language learner to be able to put together sentences which convey his or her personal intentions. We wanted to find out what kinds of language classroom instructional methods are prevalent in African language programs. So we asked a series of questions that deal with various teaching practices, testing practices, and other classroom activities related issues. About 82% of the respondents use both the communicative and functional approaches in their classrooms. Fewer than 9% the lecture or audio-lingual approach in conjunction with both communicative and functional approaches.

Schuh (1988, 9) laments the prevalence of "outdated audio-lingual and even grammar translation techniques" in African language programs. The fact that 100% of our respondents claim to use the functional approach and about 82% claim to use both functional and communicative approaches shows that African language instructors are moving away from the audio-lingual, lecture (in English), and grammar-translation approaches which were most common in the 1980s.

We wanted to find out if the respondents do non-drill language activities in class during which students are guided to "express themselves" in communicative situations (e.g., games, simulations, role playing, etc.). All respondents indicated that they give their students communicative activities to practice using the language (Table 2.6). Only about 27% use translation in addition to communicative activities. What this finding indicates is that a greater percentage of African language instructors are encouraging their students to use the language in a meaningful way, even though most of the available textbooks are filled with grammar translation exercises, fill-in-the-blanks, and patterned drills activities.

As any student quickly learns, a teacher's statement about what he or she is trying to accomplish in any given classroom does not necessarily coincide with that teacher's goals. A teacher's goals are best discovered by inspecting the kinds of tests he or she administers. For this reason, we asked our respondents if they tested "communicative competence." We attempted to clarify this term by stating that we wanted to know if language instructors are giving tests that require students to convey meaning in a non-memorized conversational situation. All respondents indicated a move from grammar translation and fill-in-the-blanks tests toward testing the communicative competence of their students through writing and speaking.

	1	2	3	4	5	6	7	8	9	10	11	12	13	14	15
Role play	•	•	•	•	•	•		•	•	•	•	•		•	•
Communicative Activities	•	•	•	•	•	•	•	•	•	•	•	•	•	•	•
Translation	•		•				•								

Table 2.6. Types of learning activities.

The use of the target language in foreign language instruction is a topic which is quite frequently discussed in recent foreign language education literature, particularly with regard to the lower level language courses. We wanted to discover the percentage of all African language classrooms that use the target language that is used in all African language classrooms. Our data shows that, on average, 81% of respondents of the target language at the elementary level, 84% at the intermediate level, and about 86% at the advanced level.

The percentage at the advanced level is a little disturbing since one would expect that advanced students would be able to use and understand the language a lot more than elementary and intermediate students. Nevertheless, the findings show that the majority of African language instructors now use more of the target language in the classrooms compared with the 1960s, 1970s, and the 1980s when it was more common to teach the language in English. There is no doubt that a series of NDEA VI (Title VI) OPI workshops and thus by the African Language Teachers Association in the late 1980s and early 1990s for African language instructors have contributed to the progress indicated by these findings.

Closely related to the issue of using the target language in a language course is the question of whether or not any of the other courses in African language programs are taught in African languages. We wanted to know if, for example, after the advanced level language course, students have the opportunity to continue learning their respective African languages by taking courses (such as literature) that are taught in an African language. All respondents indicated that there are no non-language courses at their institutions that are specifically taught in any African language in the U.S. Literary texts in the language could be

%	1	2	3	4	5	6	7	8	9	10	11	12	13	14	15	Avg.
1st year	75	65	50	75	75	80	70	70	70	75	70	70	65	90	80	72
2nd year	85	75	66	75	85	85	75	80	75	90	80	80	75	90	85	80
3rd year	90	75	66	80	90	90	80	90	80	95	90	90	75	90	90	85

Table 2.7. Percentage of classrooms using the target language.

made available to a very few students who study the language up to the third or fourth year levels. Although the students read and discuss the texts themselves, they read much less about general issues of literature. In most cases, such texts are used only for comprehension activities.

Content-based instruction is also frequently discussed in foreign language education literature. As a result, we wanted to know where the field of African language pedagogy stands concerning content-based instruction. We asked respondents to describe the type of content that is incorporated into their language instruction. All indicated that they incorporate cultural content that is grammar- or function-driven at the elementary and inter-mediate levels. One respondent noted that

> the elementary and intermediate materials are designed to stimulate conversation practices, particularly grammatical structures. Cultural topics are chosen, promoting the use of particular grammar but the main emphasis is on conversation, vocabulary building, and introduction to aspects of culture. I would say that the focus in the lessons is on language, not on culture per se. That is, there is no systematic attempt in the culture lessons to cover all aspects of the cultural subject. Likewise, tests do not cover a student's comprehensive knowledge of content.

This particular respondent echoes the sentiment of all the other respondents.

About 27% added that they incorporate content based instruction on students' research interests and needs at the advanced level. There is no indication that learners' needs or research interests are incorporated at the elementary and intermediate levels. The problem is that, since most African language learners do not have the opportunity to study the language up to the advanced level, by the time most African language instructors decide to incorporate learners' interests and research needs, most learners would have left the program because most African language students usually study the language up to the intermediate level before they graduate (see Arasanyin, et al. 1996).

Finally, in order to obtain general information about what respondents feel are major problems confronting African language instruction in the U.S., we asked them to describe these problems in their own words. They listed several problems, including the following:

a. There is a lack of instructional materials, (both textbooks, dictionaries) and instructional technology materials, and teaching aids.
b. Programs are suffering from low enrollments which affect institutional support.
c. Most teachers have not had enough training as language teachers. Consequently, they are ill-prepared to adapt poor materials or create their own. Also, they have little understanding of language acquisition and how to approach it effectively in the classroom.
d. There is a lack of motivation on the part of the students.
e. There is a lack of commitment. Students are generally not encouraged by their family or institution to study African languages.

One respondent, out of frustration, said:

Our problem is not in the classroom, but rather outside the

classroom. We are still victims of colonial language policy—too few students are attracted by African languages. African languages have not achieved the recognition they deserve, and thus don't attract the students, and therefore, don't get the financial support.

At this respondent's institution, there are only two faculty members in their African language program and there is no lecturer position. They depend on money from the federal government to pay graduate students to teach part-time. This situation is typical of many African language programs (they lack money to hire qualified language instructors). The majority of those who teach African languages on a regular basis are untrained TAs with little or no supervision. Most programs cannot afford to hire full-time language faculty. If there is no money to hire qualified professionals for the regular language programs, it seems implausible to expect money for creating special courses or focus classes to integrate language study and subject-matter courses. In many African language programs, there is only one person in charge of one language or sometimes many languages.

Limited access to appropriate materials (whether written, oral, visual, or multimedia) is also a common problem in African language instruction. Only the most commonly taught African languages such as Hausa, Swahili, and Yoruba can boast of metalanguage books for special terminology in other disciplines.

In spite of all of the problems listed above, it is important to know that African language instruction in the U.S. has come a long way. About a decade ago, Schuh (1988, 8) noted that, "No African language at all has an intermediate or advanced textbook, good or bad." But currently, at least Swahili and Yoruba can boast about books at those levels. There are now many video and computer-assisted language learning materials for some African languages (see chapter seven). More dictionaries are currently being written for Hausa, Swahili, and Yoruba. With the inception of an annual ALTA conference in 1997, the professionalization of African language teachers is now becoming a reality. In chapter eight, we will show the different ways in which ALTA is attempting to address the problems listed above.

CHAPTER THREE

Focus on Teaching

1. BACKGROUND

As we looked at the perspectives for African language development in chapter two, we indicated that teachers and students play crucial roles in the development of a credible program. We talked about the different ways teaching is done in the Title VI and non-Title VI programs. We also discussed students interests in African languages. In this chapter, we will focus on the African language teacher as part of the perspective for African language program development in the twenty-first century.

In chapters one and two, we also discussed three types of instruction in African language programs. We noted that there are programs with a tenured or tenure-track faculty member who may be in-charge of instruction and programming and who may occasionally teach one or more language classes. In these cases where the faculty member's main function is to direct the program, the role of the teacher is relegated to part-time staff or teaching assistants. In the third type of instruction we noted an absence of faculty at both the teaching and programming levels where the bulk of the work is done instead by a supervised or unsupervised tutor. The immediate supervisor of the instructor is often the head of the unit (as department head or program director) or a faculty member in a non-language department (history, political science, anthropology).

Regardless of their status, all those who assume the roles of teacher or facilitator face the same challenges in teaching a foreign language, a challenge that can be exacerbated when the language has features that are alien to the learner's first language. African languages, as taught in the U.S., fit this description. To address this, we will first attempt to answer the question: What is the profile of an African language teacher? A second question for focusing on the learner will be answered in chapter four.

2. TEACHER PROFILE

Ideally, a foreign language teacher should be a trained teacher who understands the principles of language instruction, language teaching, and language classroom management. It is unfortunate that some programs pay more attention to a teacher's language proficiency and ability to handle the grammar of the language than the teacher's experience in teaching a foreign language, teacher training skills, and understanding of the culture of the language. An ability to speak a language fluently does not automatically imply that one has the ability to teach it. There is more that goes on in a language classroom than simply instructing the students in the target language. It is also unfortunate that we require qualifications in the teaching of the commonly taught languages, but we lower the standards when it comes to the less commonly taught languages. Many African language programs have teachers from other disciplines (e.g., history, geography, anthropology, etc.) teaching the language often unsupervised. The quality of instruction is often left unchecked. It is unclear how such a program can be expected to last more than a couple of years. Both Title VI and non-Title VI programs share the same criticism here and, therefore, should be challenged to demand from their institutions that their language classes be managed more effectively. They should have both a programmer and an instructor who is professional and knowledgeable of the best teaching methods and learning strategies. Until that is done, there is no way these language programs can preserve their integrity. The field of African languages cannot be expected to develop if its guardians are not paying attention to the profile of the teachers they put into the classroom.

3. THE BUSINESS OF TEACHING

The business of language instruction has both realistic and unrealistic expectations. It is unrealistic for example, to expect students in a classroom setting to achieve a full native speaker's proficiency in the language. It is equally unrealistic for students to expect the teacher to make them native speakers of the language or to provide them with all of the learning strategies and skills needed to master the target language. What a teacher can do is encourage each student to develop his or her own learning strategy and skills. Effective instruction must have accurate information presented by the teacher, a strong teacher-student guide component, a supervised practice component, and a dual (teacher-student and student-teacher) assessment component. Guidance is important in instruction because no student learns all that is taught during a single exposure. Students will make errors and frequently remain unaware that they have made them. The interactive process of a student attempting to apply new knowledge, an instructor correcting and guiding him or her, and a student attempting to learn are the most important aspects of instruction. Teaching and learning should be done in a partnership between the teacher and the student since the teacher cannot make students learn if they are not ready or willing to. Because the teacher is assumed to be the guardian of knowledge, there are certain expectations among students. A teacher must:

- have extensive knowledge of the target language and its culture.
- demonstrate language-teaching ability and experience.
- be realistic (i.e., know students' abilities, provide learning materials within the students' ability to absorb and use).
- facilitate learning in the most efficient way (i.e., help students develop student-centered learning).

With this in mind, we may ask How do teachers go about the business of teaching and learning African languages? There are two useful models for this: teacher-centered and student-centered. Many programs that requires at least five hours of classroom instruction per week tend to use the teacher-centered mode of instruction, which is the traditional way of teaching any subject in a structured classroom.

In the teacher-centered approach, control over what is to be learned and how it should be learned rests squarely on the teacher's shoulders. The curriculum and syllabus often rely heavily on the textbook, and the instructional process is restricted to the material in the textbook. In language instruction, there is a tendency to focus on the acquisition of the major linguistic aspects of the language as described in existing grammars. Teachers favor this mode because they take control over the comprehension of the general subject-matter, and decide when to move from one stage to another. Class goals reflect the teacher's goals with specific objectives for each class meeting. Such goals are often marked by a very rigid syllabus with a strict insistence from the teacher to follow it to the letter and to complete it at a given period of time. The teacher is, for the most part, viewed as the *expert.*

Although teachers may favor this mode because it makes it easier to manage a class, it may discourage motivated students from actively participating in the class activities. It may also reduce the way students contribute to the general knowledge of the subject matter. It is important to remember that each student brings personal experiences to the language class that can be exploited for the benefit of the other students.

A limited student participation model is characterized as a lecture. Language teaching should not be done in a lecture format. A lecture approach assumes that the teacher is the expert and the teaching techniques are restrictive, skills-oriented, and very systematic. That is, the teacher brings to the class specific models of knowledge and ways of learning and then work toward making sure that the students fit into that particular model. For example in the teaching of Kiswahili, if the teacher brings to the class a grammar-based model, he or she will aim at making the students experts in the analysis of the grammatical features of the language and, by osmosis, develop proficiency which is free from grammatical errors. This is very much the traditional model, one that was used in the training of students to do language translations but not to use the language for communicative purposes. A teacher-centered approach may also force students to accommodate the teacher's suggested model of learning. Often, in this model, the students' goals and objectives of learning may be radically different from the teacher's model. Consequently in the teacher-centered model, the students' goals and objectives may receive low priority or may be completely overlooked.

In contrast, a student-centered model is non-restrictive by the mere fact that the student's involvement and participation greatly influences decisions made by the teacher. The teacher's role is limited to that of facilitator and resource person while the students bring to class specific broad knowledge that is relevant to what they want to learn. The teacher takes the responsibility for coordinating this body of knowledge through class activities and designs a learning environment which facilitates an efficient way of learning the target language. By including the students in this process, the teacher builds on their background knowledge which the teacher then establishes as a common foundation for learning and understanding the various concepts necessary to learn the target language and gain cultural proficiency. In other words, the teacher does not seek or expect specific behavior across the student body just as he or she would not expect an exact answer to a question asked in class. Rather, the teacher encourages student participation, creativity, and the ability to govern the information disseminated. In this way, the teacher provides room for guided understanding and acquisition of the target language without imposing a rigid structure.

What are we, then, suggesting to the teacher? We suggest that the focus be learning and not *teaching*. The learning process must, therefore, be meaningful to the student. In learning, the student is central and each student has a part to play in the learning process. This is not an easy job for a teacher because individual students differ in many ways. The teacher must recognize and respond to those differences. Student variables include: (1) demographics (age, gender, cultural background, and educational background)—often a class may have a mixture of graduate and undergraduate students with the undergraduates subcategorized according to the stage of their college residency); (2) language learning experience (some students may come with much experience having learned another foreign language); (3) degree of preexisting competence in the target language (prior exposure through travel or actual classroom learning); (4) learning style (e.g., rote memorization); (5) personality type (e.g., introvert vs. extrovert); (6) motivation (cultural interest, language requirement, prior exposure, immediate use of the language such as travel or employment).

An awareness of these differences commits the teacher to a student-centered teaching to facilitate student-centered learning. In student-centered teaching, the teacher will (1) solicit information from his or her students, (2) make expectations and class assumptions explicit at the onset, (3) provide different kinds of learning activities (such as cooperative, individual, computer assisted learning or active, interactive, fact-finding, and information packaging), and (4) provide each student with appropriate counseling and feedback concerning his or her day to day progress in the class.

Although these variables are not unique to African language classes, recognizing them is vital in African language instruction because of the mere fact that, unlike commonly taught languages and like many less commonly taught languages, African languages pose special problems to students who may have been exposed to Indo-European languages in high school and who may expect to find some similarities or major differences in learning the specific African language.

Despite the challenges that students face, African languages attract a sizable number of students at the college level, at least at the elementary and intermediate levels. It seems, therefore, inevitable that as teachers, we need to be aware of the teacher-centered and student-centered modes and make a conscious effort to adopt a strategy that not only pays attention to learner's goals and needs but also encourages students to take full responsibility for their learning. The partnership we are suggesting here is one that is equitable and does not weigh more heavily on the teacher (in teaching responsibilities) or the student (in learning responsibilities). A balanced approach is vital in order to deal effectively with (a) a coherent cultural component, (b) a context-based grammar, (c) a context-based vocabulary, and (d) a systematic approach to interactive learner participation.

4. TEACHING FOR LEARNING

As much as it is for the students, the first day of classes for any teacher is a blind date. It is telling that teachers prefer the easy way out of this complicated situation by adopting a teacher-centered mode or a restrictive type of instruction. In this way, the teacher feels he or she is in control of the situation. For most teachers, it takes about three weeks to ease tension in the classroom. In the event that this is not accomplished in that time, there often result complaints from both the students and the teacher, each criticizing the other's performance. In such an environment, it is impossible to teach for learning as to learn for the purpose of developing sustainable proficiency. Thus, an effective teacher should seek ways to turn a blind date into a long lasting relationship that is full of adventure, exploration, enthusiasm, motivation, and (most of all) creativity and discovery.

When Teaching for Learning (TL), the teacher should be aware that the class will consist of individuals who share very little in common in terms of goals and needs. Therefore, the levels of motivation, and learning skills will be different. TL requires that the teacher assume the role of a facilitator and one who unifies the group. Without a unified group, *teaching for learning* cannot be realized without adversely affecting the individual student's goals and expectations. Students need to get a feel for what the teacher can do to enhance their learning process. The teacher needs to get a feel for the students cumulative or individual needs, skills, and levels of motivation in order to devise a teaching plan that can make teaching and learning enjoyable and less tedious and demanding. Learning a language should be like building a house, where each accomplishment brings excitement and expectations to add a new layer each time.

The ingredients for effective TL include good preparation, evaluation, and feedback. This is not asked of the teacher only, but of the students too. Both the teacher and the students must go to class fully prepared for the materials to be covered that day. A teacher's class preparation includes having an outline of the areas to be covered, detailed notes on the subject, and a list of activities which will be incorporated into the lesson indicating at what point each activity should be introduced. Most importantly, the lesson plan should be flexible enough to allow for changes if the continuous evaluation indicates that learning is not taking place. Ideally, the teacher should have a backup plan for each planned lesson, one that can easily repair what the first plan

65

failed to do to impart learning. The students should prepare themselves by reviewing materials taught in previous classes or by reviewing specific parts of the intended lesson plan (e.g., grammar, vocabulary, cultural notes).

Dictated by the African culture, each class should start with a familiarization stage which involves exchanging greetings, and a pep-talk (short, informal conversations on the day's events such as the weather or any aspect of social life that the teacher or students want to bring up). This is a cultural discourse requirement following from the way native speakers of many African languages go about meeting other people, and it is a pre-requisite for conducting daily business.

The familiarization stage need not be teacher-guided (with teacher asking student X to converse with student Y), rather it should be student-initiated as well as student-managed. This activity can be done in pairs or the teacher can require that the students get out of their seats and meet at least three other students, exchange greetings, and then chat for a few minutes before settling down to the days planned lesson. The teacher is advised to exercise his or her role as facilitator and evaluator. The opening of the day's lesson could consist of be a feedback on the evaluation of the students' initial activity. It is a good time to reinforce what was learned well and to repair any learning cracks. TL requires that there be a few minutes in which what has already been learned is reviewed in order to strengthen the foundation on which new material will be added. The TL goal should be to build a strong structure that will remain strong beyond the basic stages of acquiring the target language.

TL requires also that the teacher teach the language not the textbook. In teacher-centered or restrictive instruction, teachers tend to focus more on the available texts. Consequently, students expend their energy learning the text material and preparing to be tested on just that. This is not learning; it is a transfer of text from paper to a temporary storage location; the student's brain. Teaching the textbook instead of the language forces students to learn the language by memorizing words and the available patterns for the formation of phrases and sentences. Consequently, proficiency is short lived because of the limitations imposed on the students by this mode of teaching and learning. In TL, the textbook should serve as a teaching aid, a tool that students can use outside of the classroom to reinforce the classroom TL.

A well-balanced TL methodology must therefore adopt a non-restrictive mode of instruction in order to deal effectively with a coherent cultural component, a context based grammar, a context based vocabulary, and a systematic approach for interactive learner participation.

5. LANGUAGE LEARNING GOALS

Language learners ultimately want to develop effective communication skills in the target language. It is important for the learner to attain the three levels of proficiency, speaking, reading/comprehension, and composition. It is not, therefore, enough to learn only the structure of the target language but rather to understand the contributions of pragmatics and the culture. As we will discuss later, "culture" is the heart of language learning whether the ultimate goal is to fulfill general education requirements (often the goal of undergraduate language study) or to successfully and effectively communicate at a native speaker level (primarily for graduate students who will use the language for research in the target language).

Antonia Schleicher and Lioba Moshi

The learning that fits these goals has to distinguish between learning the language and learning *about* the language. The biggest challenge for African language teachers is how to teach for learning, especially when the goal is to teach declarative knowledge. The challenge is exacerbated by the marginalization of procedural knowledge with its pressure on teachers to make the teaching of a language super academic, with exams and tests as the major means of measuring student's academic achievement. Consequently, language teachers see their teaching which embraces procedural knowledge as distinct from teaching for learning. There is evidence from human behavior in communication that procedural knowledge is not classroom taught, but can be acquired from our environment. We certainly use it in acquiring our first language.

Based on our earlier discussion of teacher-centered and learner-centered instruction, it is clear that learner centered instruction makes extensive use of procedural knowledge. By developing what a learner brings to the learning environment, the teacher inadvertently embraces the principles of procedural knowledge. Consequently, the emphasis is on *teaching* the language and not on providing information *about* the language. After all when a child acquires his or her language, knowledge about the language is not part of the learning process, per se, although it is fair to say that it is reserved as subconscious knowledge, retrieved only at a later stage and when it is needed. Language teachers ought to take clues from the observation, that teaching about the language is secondary at best and mostly unnecessary at elementary and intermediate levels where the emphasis is learning to communicate using the target language rather than learning to analyze the language. The latter should be reserved for linguistics and literature classes.

The main pitfall in teaching about the language is in the

68

excessive use of textbooks. As noted earlier, African languages are in dire need of good textbooks. The suggestion that the field must give teachers a better choice of teaching materials does not imply that teachers are handicapped at present because of a lack of these text materials. Doing so would imply that the African language teacher is dependent on textbook materials for teaching. Teaching for learning calls for creativity on the part of the teacher, both in teaching and using teaching resources. Textbooks, like all other teaching resources, are merely tools for TL. With a careful plan and guidance, students can construct their own ways of learning as well as knowledge schemas with or without textbooks. Students' abilities to construct knowledge enables them to appropriate knowledge using existing knowledge schema.

For a teacher, recognizing the existence of such a framework in the mind of a learner will enable him or her to know the conditions that are conducive to learning, to relative ease or difficulty in absorbing new material, and how to assist the student to develop a systematic way of learning the target language for effective communication and not just to fulfill an academic requirement. This follows from the learner-centered theory which stresses that it is the learner who determines what, when, and how to learn (see also Krashen 1991). The theory is based on the recognition of a learners' ability to learn. The focus is not on teaching but on learning since the teacher's role is to facilitate learning rather than to subordinate learning to teaching. As a facilitator, the learning process is outside the teacher's control as he or she organizes the information and appropriates knowledge to enable the learner to learn effectively.

With learner-centered teaching comes the primacy of learner-comprehension. Because learner performance is the primary process through which acquisition takes place, the learner must understand what the communicative task is before attempting to perform. For example, in the teaching of vocabulary, exercises that help the students to recognize vocabulary items are better than those which require students to recall specific vocabulary items. This is why it makes sense to learn vocabulary in context. The same is true for any other aspect of language learning: grammar, sound, word formation, etc. Students will learn better and even remember more if sounds are taught in context and by contrasting them with others in context. Without comprehension, we cannot expect the learner to cultivate confidence that will play a key role in the full acquisition of the language, nor can we expect the learner to develop techniques for comprehensive input and output.

For comprehensive input to work, the learner needs to know that his or her interpretations are correct. It is, therefore, important for the teacher to move from the *known* to the *unknown*. In other words, he or she must know what the learner already knows or has successfully learned before moving to new material. The avenues for this are *feedback* and *evaluation*. Whereas evaluation (through testing) serves the academic purpose of the language class, feedback is equally important in that it provides the learner and the teacher with a sense of whether learning is or is not taking place. Feedback should be seen as a dual process which enhances the acquisition process. Learner feedback is an integral part in learner-centered language learning process. Consequently, learner feedback should be a continual process, an integral part of the curriculum and, ultimately, the syllabus. Feedback and evaluation are not necessarily always structured. Any activity request from the teacher to a student or a student to another student is a form of feedback and evaluation.

6. TEACHING LANGUAGE FOR CRITICAL THINKING

Despite theories on discourse production and analysis which have implications for language use, critical thinking is often eliminated from the process of language learning. Too few students, teachers, supervisors, and college administrators view the language class-room as a place for critical thinking. This can be explained by the fact that language learning in a classroom setting is often artificial and divorced from real life. It is mind boggling to expect students to remember what they learn in the classroom when very few or no real life issues are brought to bear in any of the contexts exploited in the classroom.

The business of language teaching for learning has to embrace critical thinking, defined here as reflective thinking which focuses on deciding what to believe or do in a given context. The business of language teaching cannot ignore critical thinking because of the nature of language and communication. In effective com-munication, we emphasize the ability to consider one's thinking in order to recognize its strength and weaknesses and, as a result, to re-think in improved ways. The critical question is what does it mean when we say "thinking about one's thinking?"

Thinking about one's thinking involves the ability to identify the basic elements of thought (purpose, question, information, assumption, interpretation, concepts, implications, point of view) and assess these elements using universal intellectual criteria and standards (clarity, accuracy, precision, relevance, depth, breadth, and logic). Of course, there are those who will read this and say that such a view belongs to, disciplines that deal with theory and philosophies not language learning. But what we need to remember is that there is no discipline which does not need language. Language is central to human behavior and in the process of learning it, the learner has to sharpen those tools that will be needed in each and every area. Thus, in a language classroom, the learner should be engaged in the discussion of the same issues he or she will discuss in other classes. Language learning means learning how to communicate on any subject matter.

Teaching language for critical thinking eliminates learning prescribed frames and patterns through drills, eliminates the artificiality of language learning while it brings in contextualization, coherence, and discourse continuity. It focuses on conscious language learning rather than memorized patterns for the purpose of academic feedback and evaluation. Critical thinking in language teaching and learning involves asking questions which are not designed for problem solving; the intention is not to ask a student to solve a problem but rather to think aloud. It is important to realize that critical thinking precedes problem solving, making the solution to a problem a small part of the critical thinking process.

In language teaching for critical thinking, a student will spend time thinking about the answer before he or she provides the answer. If the language learning process is not designed for critical thinking, the student will only be required to provide pre-learned frames or patterns which emerge from luck, creativity, or independent input. Of course, a student's performance can be evaluated as having failed to demonstrate critical thinking. It is important for the teacher[3] to guide the students to use critical thinking in their language learning endeavors and refrain from parroting. It is easy for a teacher to notice when a student is asking a question of others without reasoning it out or with no

3. As a facilitatior.

intention to believe or act on the answer. It is reasonable to expect students to ask a question and, while they try to reason it out, make mistakes. It is also possible for a student to fail to ask a question or respond to one. The teacher's role should be to offer guidance and to facilitate critical thinking. This can be done through asking questions or making suggestions.

Critical thinking in a language classroom should be designed to combine the course content with applications within the discipline, across disciplines, and in real life. It is a mistake to make students view language learning as "language stuff" that has no implication or applicability to reality. When we require literature, African studies, or business to learn a language, we do not expect them to learn only a set of language rules, vocabulary items. Rather, we expect them to use rules of grammar and vocabulary as the foundation and a springboard from which they can launch the main tasks of communicating effectively as context demands. Such demands require not only a high level of creativity, but also critical thinking. The students will be expected to be able to ask and answer questions in a spontaneous manner (which is an art in effective communication) and not from a memorized set of answers or list of vocabulary items or phrases (which is considered parroting). Language is not just words and phrases. It is content and context. Language depends on concepts and concept learning, both of which are integral parts of cognitive development. It is a mistake to assume that students' preferred beliefs and assumptions are out of bounds in a language classroom. The sooner they learn how to explore them in the target language, the better they will be in developing their communicative skills which greatly depend on how well they can think critically.

In summary, critical thinking goes beyond the information given by the teacher or a textbook. To enable students to use

73

critical thinking in the classroom, teachers, who are facilitators and guides, should refrain from teaching a set of given items (i.e., the textbook) and teach the language. Teachers should stop viewing a language classroom as a place where you find unique answers to unique questions. There are no unique questions or unique answers in any discipline, and it should not be expected in language learning. Once a problem or situation has been posed, students will only be expected to provide a variety of solutions. The instructor must ask the students to justify their answers or solutions in terms of reason rather than as learned phrases or vocabulary items.

Because critical thinking involves disposing the mind in a given way for reasoning, considering, judging, and evaluating, language students have to keep sight of the overall picture of the situation from which to draw the ideas needed for a successful communicative act. They need to develop an independent way of solving a problem, explaining a situation, offering advice, suggesting appropriate measures. The language classroom should not be viewed any differently than other classrooms where students learn to think critically. It is only when critical thinking is fully integrated into the language learning process that we can expect students to *learn how to learn* a language and view the learning of a language as a sustained effort and a life long endeavor. Sustainable, lifelong learning can be attained by:

- selecting concepts that can serve as a foundation for the students to think in a critical manner and to structure activities around these concepts;
- providing (if necessary) key vocabulary and important phrases which the students may need to express themselves well;
- providing examples or assignments that demonstrate how a

specific concept can be applied to students' daily lives, the importance of asking questions, keeping a journal or records of events;

- building a term goal to cultivate critical reading, writing, speaking and listening skills of the students. This can and should, if possible, be based on the skills already acquired.
- Encouraging students to speak in full sentences and to elaborate what they have said by rephrasing or by giving concrete examples to help the rest of the class to understand both the content and context;
- promoting the skill of incorporating one's emotions into what they are articulating in order to enhance the affective dimension of critical thinking. One's emotions will bring to the discussion intellectual courage, humility, and fair-mindedness;
- teachers themselves exhibiting critical thinking skills in the examples that may be selected as a start-up kit. These skills can be shown in a question answer technique, where the students are guided to ask each other or the teacher leading or deductive questions.

CHAPTER FOUR

Focus on the African Language Learner

1. BACKGROUND

In chapter three, we discussed two types of teaching modes: teacher-centered and student-centered. We indicated that students or learners, should be central to and not a by-product of language instruction because each student has a part to play in the learning process which includes an understanding of the language, its speakers, and their culture. Learning must be meaningful to the student for it to be considered a means toward communicative competence in the target language.

When we talk about "the learner" we are talking about learning. Learning can be defined as a "permanent change in a behavioral tendency and is the result of reinforced practice" (Kimble and Garmezy 1963, 133). We can link this definition to that of teaching in that "teaching" implies showing or helping someone to learn, giving instructions, guiding in the study of something, providing with knowledge, causing to know or understand.

We can, therefore, talk about the learner as one who acquires knowledge and learning as a process of acquiring and retaining information or skills. Retention implies storage systems, memory, and cognitive organization of the acquired information. Thus, learning involves active, conscious focus on some subject matter. Learning involves practice which may sometimes be reinforced by someone other than the learner, a role ascribed to the teacher. This is why learning and teaching are mutually exclusive even though learning does not always require a human teacher. Teaching is guiding and facilitating learning, enabling the learner to learn, setting the conditions for learning. The teacher's understanding of how the learner learns is determined by his or her philosophy of learning, teaching style, approach, methods, and classroom techniques.

Before we elaborate on these concepts and show the implications to learners of an African language, let's first discuss the profile of the typical African language student.

2. STUDENT PROFILE

Who is a student of African languages? This is a question asked all the time at institutions where African languages are taught, partly because most Americans consider studying an African language pretty exotic. It is also assumed that only disciplines like history, anthropology, sociology, and linguistics will provide a reservoir of students interested in African languages. It is always a surprise to many when they find out that African language programs attract students from both the sciences and the humanities. Thus the answer to the question, who is a student of African language, does not lie in disciplines but rather in the goals of each individual student who chooses to learn an African language at the college level.

Those of us who have been teaching African languages for a while can attest to the fact that students who come to our classes have varied interests and diverse reasons for doing so. These may include curiosity, language requirement credit, a desire for a cultural or cross-cultural experience or link, the need for language skills for research, and other special needs such as developing basic communicative competence for a business trip or to work with an international organization.

Students with these needs and goals bring to an African language class varying concerns and needs which they expect to be met. These include to learn the language well enough to use it with a native speaker and to develop learning skills which are easily transferable to other languages or disciplines.

Students who enroll in African language classes because of curiosity are generally interested in finding out how the language and its culture are different from their first language and culture. They will, therefore, be extremely motivated and interested in knowing more about the people who speak the language. Student for whom sole motivation is college credit for a language requirement, the main interest will be in securing a good grade regardless of whether the learning process takes place or not. Such students make TL (teaching for learning) very difficult to implement. Students in search of a cultural experience or link come to the African language class with high expectations of learning as much as possible about the culture and about the speakers. They are less interested in detailed language and grammar explanations. Questions about the culture tend to predominate, a phenomenon that can take up a lot of class time, if not checked.

TL can exploit the situation if the teacher understands how to handle a class with diverse interests and different levels of motivation. Student-centered or non-restrictive instruction can resolve most of these management problems since the student is made responsible for his or her learning. Classroom activities and projects can be directed toward the specific student interests allowing students to learn as much as they would like to in the areas of their interest they acquire the basic language training to enable them to work independently on their projects.

Students seeking to use a language as a research tool are generally more mature students usually in graduate school. As such they have a clearer goal which is both knowledge and function based. The primary focus tends to be on understanding the grammar, acquisition of general and specific vocabulary items, and fluency in the language. Equally motivated are those students who come to an African language class as preparation for special and immediate needs. Usually such students are in a hurry to learn the language. The classic example is that of a student who requests the language because he or she will be traveling to Africa within weeks of the request. Such a student usually assumes that he or she can learn enough of the language in just a short period to become partially functional. They appear highly motivated as well as interested in specific aspects of the language. TL will work well for this group of learners because it gives the students maximum opportunity to be involved in the planning of what to learn and how it should be learned. The teacher, as we noted earlier, is only a facilitator. This means that the teacher sees himself or herself as a resource person for the students and that the students bring to class knowledge that is relevant to what they want to learn. The teacher's responsibility is to coordinate that body of knowledge and to help the student design a learning environment which will facilitate an effective and efficient way through which TL can take place.

TL is also an approach that seeks to develop a common foundation for learning and understanding the various concepts transmitted through language. Encouraging student participation sends a message to the students that each student in the class is unique and his or her contribution, however small, is useful to the whole class. By accepting these various responses from students, the teacher will likewise accept the different environments and backgrounds of the student.

TL espouses the importance of a teaching learning partnership between the teacher and the students. The students must want to learn, the teacher must be prepared to provide the needed learning guide. By saying that the teacher is a facilitator, it does not mean that the teacher is not an expert in the field. It only means that the teacher should not be the only person working in the class. The classroom environment should be one in which the teacher and the students are both working very hard to achieve their goals but also in which the student and the student alone is in control of his or her learning.

We have painted the picture here as if the TL challenge is dual. We must, however, emphasize that the teacher's challenge should be viewed in light of how he or she needs to accommodate students with diverse interests as discussed here. He or she must be able to identify the motivation levels that students bring to class. He or she must find a way to develop it (if it is non-existent), enhance it (if it is inadequate), or maintain it (if the level is reasonably adequate). Teacher preparedness is crucial and key to student preparedness for success in a TL mode of instruction. How can a teacher of African languages assist in student preparedness?

3. FOCUS ON PREPAREDNESS

First and foremost, teacher's preparedness will serve as a model for student preparedness. Being prepared to learn is essential, and if the student observes that the teacher is fully prepared to teach, tardiness will not be a factor. Having a coherent syllabus, defined goals and objectives will define for the student the path through which he or she will travel to achieve the desired proficiency. Another very crucial strategy is that which removes any illusions from the student on the teaching and learning procedures. For African languages, a teacher cannot afford to teach textual material only. The teacher must be prepared to teach the language from its culture. As such, the student will have to be prepared to learn beyond the textbook, making the textbook an accessory only. The book cannot replace the teacher. Doing so affects the student's motivation and preparedness to deal with the challenges that come with learning a language which is totally unrelated to his or her first language. When a student comes to class unprepared for these challenges, he or she may be driven to frustration and ultimately the interest to learn the mechanics of mastering the concepts, the language, and the patterns that are the foundation for his or her speaking, listening, reading/comprehension, and writing.

Being fully prepared to learn enables the student to establish attitudes towards learning and the motivation to sustain the enduring process of learning the language. This appears to be extremely important in the learning of African languages, particularly for American students. Research (Lambert 1959; Gardner 1985) shows that a learner's orientation to learning a second language is closely related to his or her overall attitude to learning and his or her motivation to learn the language. This is why the teacher's role in facilitating learning is so important.

An individual's willingness and interest to learn includes his or her willingness to interact with other learners. This can be assessed by observing the student's attitude towards his or her language learning associates, his or her interest in learning that particular African language (Swahili vs. Yoruba vs. Hausa vs. Shona vs. Zulu, etc.), and an integrated orientation toward learning the language of choice.

A student's attitude to learning an African language will reflect his or her overall evaluation of the way he or she is being instructed. This can be assessed by his or her attitude towards the teacher, and the course outline, goals, and objectives. Motivation will reflect the student's attitudes, desires, and effort to learn the language of choice and the attraction to this particular language. Often the attraction has nothing to do with the language itself, but rather external factors including teacher's reputation, other students' evaluations, and reports about that particular class. Thus, to facilitate learning by working on the student's motivation, the teacher has to evaluate the student's attitude toward learning the language, the desire to learn the language, and the motivational intensity.

The teacher can also help the learner to identify important elements to be learned from the *less salient elements*, including the sequence in which they should be learned. Less salient elements can be learned as background to the more salient elements. This will be among the language learning strategies that are deemed essential in facilitating learning and which we can define as techniques that individuals use to facilitate learning and to improve skills. The teacher can adopt what is known as *Strategy Inventory for Language Learning* (SILL). This was designed (Oxford 1986) as a self-report assessment which determines the extent to which an individual learner can use analytic investigation of language learning strategies. Five of the factors identified (Oxford, Nyikos, and Crookall 1987) and which are useful for the African language learner include general study habits, functional practice, speech and communicative meaning, studying and practicing independently, and memory devices. I would also add to this list the ability to use culture effectively as a means to achieve sustainable communicative skills. This last suggestion includes Chamot's (1990) socio-affective strategy.

Many learners of foreign languages bring to class a substantial amount of anxiety. To facilitate learning, the student has to develop self-confidence. Self-confidence is a positive component of learning while anxiety is a negative component. Negativism breeds attitude problems which can act as a deterrent to motivation. Lack of self-confidence, as noted by Clément, et al. (1977, 1980, 1985, 1994), affects measures of proficiency in second language acquisition. Only when students are able to, overcome anxiety by building self-confidence can they maximally prepare for what they want to learn, develop effective communication skills (particularly oral skills), and retain what they have learned in the African language of their choice. This is exceptionally important for English L1 or L2 students learning an African language.

Because we tend to think teaching and learning are mutually exclusive, we have spent extensive time demonstrating their relatedness by defining the crucial role of the teacher as a facilitator of learning. We also cautioned that the learner is, for the most part, responsible for the learning process since the teacher cannot make the learner learn. We reiterate the importance of the learners perception and attention, memory, comprehension, active learning, motivation, locus of control, transfer of learning and recognizing individual students learning differences.

Learning requires the learner to attend to certain stimuli and correctly perceive them. Perception is constantly strained by many competing stimuli. Attention may falter during instruction. Thus, the kind of instruction that is learner-centered and effective depends on presentations designed for easy and accurate perception. Once the learner has succeeded in correctly perceiving the stimuli, they will be stored for later retrieval. Organization is critical to this process of memory recall. It is extremely important for the African language teacher to show the learner how the information is or can be organized in order to aid memory recall. It may even be necessary, especially where motivation is low, to impose an organizational structure on the learning process to enhance memory recall.

The learner's job is only half done if what he or she perceives, stores, and can retrieve on demand is not interpretable and fully integrated into his or her knowledge of the world. The learner must be able to classify, apply, evaluate, and manipulate the information. For the African language learner, this task is very challenging because of the complexity of the language structure and the embodied culture. For the teacher who designs both the teaching materials and the strategies which enhance the learning process, he or she must be guided by the principles of second language acquisition (e.g., use of prior knowledge, defining and exemplifying concepts, rule application, and information paraphrasing). As noted earlier, the learning desire is largely determined by the type of teacher, presentation and activities of the particular lesson, and the interesting ways culture can be incorporated in the concepts used and information given to the learner. Activities entice the learner to participate in the learning process and to interact with others. Interaction ensures attention and helps the learner to store new knowledge and skills.

An African language learner has to be motivated to accept the challenges that come with learning a language which is radically different from his or her first or mother tongue. Proper motivation is essential to learning especially where it is intrinsic to the instruction rather than externally applied. We allude to the fact that motivation is fostered by challenge, curiosity, maintenance of attention, relevance of the material, student confidence, and student satisfaction with the lesson, particularly its structure and organization. While these are applicable to all foreign languages, they are especially crucial for African language teaching and learning in Western institutions because of the low visibility associated with the teaching of these languages on college campuses.

Although the "locus of control" (Alessi and Trollip 1991) is associated more with teaching, in a student-centered teaching mode this should be controlled by the learner. Maintenance of attention, relevance of material, confidence, and satisfaction cannot be imposed on the learner, but rather can only originate from the learner. Without doubt, all lessons exhibit a mixture of student and lesson control. The extent to which we can determine the learner's success depends on which aspects of learning are controlled by the student and which are controlled by the lesson (including the teacher).

Student, lesson, or teacher control can be limited due to the fact that most teaching and learning of African languages are done outside the continent of Africa. It is important, therefore, not to lose sight of the fact that a learner's performance in the language will reflect his or her ability to transfer the classroom knowledge to the real world. Successful transfer is ultimately the most important learner-based outcome, a sign of a mature field, which should be the ultimate goal of the African languages field development plan.

Last but not least, a focus on the learner is a focus on the individual. Any good instruction should recognize that no one student learns like another. Consequently, not all instructional methodologies, strategies, or motivational factors have a uniform effect on the learner. A learner-based instructional method is one that realizes learner diversity and is cognizant of the strategies that can bring the most impact and can motivate as well as lessen learner anxiety. This can be achieved by continuous assessment of individual differences so that learners can be matched properly and decision making on how to enhance learning can be implemented.

CHAPTER FIVE

A Goal-Based Approach to African Language Instruction

Straight, et al. stated that "opportunities for foreign language use must not only increase in number but also focus more on the specific *needs and interests* [emphasis ours] of students. Schools . . . must give students opportunities and incentives to employ their foreign language skills in new contexts" (1994, 3). Similarly, Brecht and Walton suggest that "the way language learning is characterized in school.settings may need to be compared with the *needs* [emphasis ours] of life-long learners beyond schooling" (1994, 119).

Several innovative foreign language initiatives have attempted to address these concerns. For example, all of the Content-Based Instruction (CBI) programs across the nation are based on the thesis that "learners can effectively internalize new language knowledge from rich target-language data and experiences as they focus on meaningful use of the language" (Wesche 1994, 1). In these programs (see Leaver and Stryker 1989; Brinton, et al. 1989), the language elements studied and their presentation sequence are determined by the language use needs dictated by the subject matter. This means that the language curriculum is "content-driven." In any successful CBI, students gain both content knowledge and increased language proficiency.

Other educational publications are inundated with the term CBI (Cantoni-Harvey 1987; Crandall 1987; Jurasek 1988; Leaver and Stryker 1989; Brinton, et al. 1989; Allen and Anderson 1992; Freed 1992; Crandall and Turker 1990; Snow and Brinton 1992; Short 1991; Kramsch 1988a and 1993; Watkins 1990; Straight 1990; Met 1991) but there are different existing CBI programs.

In addition to the CBI programs, there is also the Foreign Language Across the Curriculum movement (referred as FLAC, LAC, or LxC)[4] that attempts to address students' specific language needs and interests.[5] In the LAC programs, the goal may not be so much "content-based foreign language instruction" as "language-based content instruction" or "foreign language-enhanced disciplinary study" (Anderson, et al., 1993, 105). These two models attempt to help students use the language in a way that meets their needs for the language study. However, these two different programs seem to work well for some European languages such as French, German, Spanish, Russian, etc., and lately East Asian languages. On the other hand, they do not seem to work well to

---

4. In subsequent discussions, we will use LAC for all the foreign languages across curriculum program.

5. See Anderson, et al., 1993; Edwards, et al., 1984; Jurasek 1982, 1988, 1992, and 1994; Wesche 1993 and 1994; Wesche and Ready 1985; Straight 1994a and 1994b; Straight, et al., 1994, Short 1994; Klee and Metcalf 1994.

meet the needs of students of African languages and other Very Less Commonly Taught Languages (VLCTL). Hence, the Goal Based Approach was proposed to account for these languages, especially African languages.

1. WHAT IS A GOAL-BASED APPROACH?

A Goal-Based Approach (GBA) to language instruction is an approach that systematically integrates students' needs, academic interests or research interests into language instruction. GBA does not replace the communicative approach or functional approach to language learning. It is proposed to be used as a supplement to ongoing communicative and/or functional instruction. GBA, while having some of the features associated with many CBI and LAC programs, it nevertheless differs from these programs in that it is neither a foreign language enriched content instruction, nor a particular subject-matter based language instruction. It is need-based or interest-based language instruction.

GBA centers language instruction on the needs and interests of students in the context of meaningful, functional, and cooperative experiences in order to develop in students motivation and interest in the learning process. The emphasis is on working with students toward using the language, not only to perform basic functions but also to discuss topics of interest to them, academic or other. In GBA, students do not have to wait till they have acquired a minimum of three or four semesters of language proficiency before their needs are incorporated into the language instruction. Instructors do not have to wait until the advanced level before integrating students' needs into the language program.

2. RATIONALE FOR THE GOAL-BASED APPROACH

As indicated in chapter one, almost all of the African language instructors surveyed noted that they integrate students' needs and academic interests into the language instruction at the advanced level. The rationale behind the delay until the advanced level is that African language learners are not expected to be able to read authentic materials related to their specific needs and interests during the first four semesters of their language learning. The early stages are devoted to mastering the basic structures of the language. The implication of this practice is that students do not have the opportunity to use the language to express their academic or personal needs and interests until they reach the advanced level. However, waiting until the advanced level leads to the exclusion of about 70% of African language students that leave the program at the end of their fourth semester of language learning.

Similarly, if we compare the existing African language programs with the CBI/LAC programs, we will observe that there are major similarities and differences between these programs. In terms of similarities, both programs tend to wait until the advanced level before incorporating students' disciplinary interests into their language studies. For example, one of the conditions for participating students in the LAC programs both at Binghamton and St. Olaf is that students must have at least a minimum 3rd or 4th semester level of the language before they can enroll in the program. Similarly, for the 27% African language programs that incorporate students' research interests, they do so at the advanced level.

Waiting till the advanced level for students studying French,

German, Spanish, Japanese, Russian, etc. may be okay since these institutions offer degree programs and students who major in these languages there have reasons to be interested in the LAC programs. For one thing, students who major in French or Spanish, for example, have to study the language beyond the second-year level. On the other hand, to wait till the advanced level for students studying African languages where there is no degree program may not be advantageous. We need to bear in mind that about 70% of African language students are undergraduates, who in most cases do not have the opportunity to study the language at the advanced level. If African language instructors wait until students have acquired three to four semesters of the language before incorporating students' interests, chances are that they will have few or no students left to take advantage of this approach.

Notice also that both the CBI/LAC programs and existing African language programs focus on reading texts at the advanced level for advanced students. The problem this presents for African language programs is the same as described above. Most African language students cannot read authentic materials at the advanced level by the time they are ready to leave the program. This is usually at the end of 2nd or 4th semester of language learning. It is important to note that about 83% of African language students surveyed by Arasanyin, et al. (1996) said they studied a European language before enrolling in African language courses. This suggests that most of them may need only two or three semesters of African language to fulfil their language requirement or to graduate. They will just be meeting the condition to enter the LAC programs or African language advanced programs by the time they are ready to leave the university. In this case, it seems safe to conclude that the existing CBI/LAC and African languages approaches do not work for African language students who mostly participate in the language program for a period of two and four semesters.

In addition to these complexities, there are other major reasons why the existing CBI/LAC programs do not work well for African language programs. Most successful CBI/LAC programs have to have a subject-matter faculty, a language faculty or resource person, and a whole staff that oversees the programs. Some CBI programs have disciplinary courses that are specially taught in the foreign language. Financially, there is no African language program in the U.S. that can afford the luxury of having a language specialist and a subject-matter specialist to handle one course. Similarly the idea of having a special history or political science course taught in Swahili, Hausa, or Yoruba is far fetched for now.

The majority of those who teach African languages on a regular basis are untrained TAs with little or no supervision. Most African language programs cannot afford to hire full-time language faculty. If there is no money to hire qualified professionals for the regular language programs, it seems implausible to expect money for creating special courses or focus classes (aside from the regular language courses) to integrate language study and subject-matter courses. In many programs, there is only one person in charge of one language or sometimes many languages (see chapter two).

Access to appropriate materials (whether written, oral, visual, or multimedia) is also a common problem for African language instruction. Only the most commonly taught African languages such as Hausa, Swahili, and Yoruba can boast of metalanguage books for special terminology in other disciplines.

Unlike some of the CBI/LAC programs, the African language classroom may be the only opportunity for our students to use the languages since there are no other courses offered specifically using an African language as the language of instruction. Nor are there special courses that will integrate texts in African languages in a subject-matter course such as history, anthropology, political science, health care, etc.

The Goal-Based approach was proposed to supplement the communicative or functional approach to allow students to incorporate their African language study into their disciplinary courses and interests. In spite of the financial constraints, the Goal-Based Approach provides ways to motivate our students beginning from first semester to integrate their overall academic interests and needs into our language curriculum. Adopting the Goal-Based Approach in conjunction with the communicative approaches will ensure that African language learners will learn beyond: (a) the structure of the language; (b) being able to perform basic functions in the language; (c) the cultural content that are vocabulary or grammar driven.

Every student in the class participates in the learning of the language and in the specific application of the knowledge of the language to their individual needs. Students are encouraged, from the very beginning of their language instruction, to be aware of the relationship between the language they are learning and their own reasons for enrolling in the language courses. Since most students have reasons (beyond fulfilling a language requirement), for enrolling in an African language course, they therefore benefit from GBA.

3. FEATURES OF THE GOAL-BASED APPROACH

The features of the Goal-Based Approach are based on the principles of language learning framework proposed in Brecht and Walton (1995)[6]. The fundamental feature of GBA is that language learning must be personalized in order to meet the needs and interests of each learner. It is an individualized, learning-centered (as opposed to teaching-centered), and learner's need-focused curriculum that holds to a conception of the active learner, of the classroom as a community, and of teachers who learn and learners who teach. It presents a learning environment in which the instructor is a co-learner and a resource who shares power with the students and allows them to make choices. The instructor becomes a learner with the students as curriculum decisions are made jointly.

In this approach, the teacher's role is to provide a content-rich environment and to provide engaging, hands-on, active learning activities that meet the interests and talents of the students. Students collaborate with each other in the learning process and, thus, learning becomes a social act.

It is not uncommon to experience conflicts of needs, goals, and objectives between instructors and students in a typical African language classroom. At a recent African linguistics conference, Antonia Folarin-Schleicher attended a talk that was presented jointly by an African language instructor and one of his students. During the presentation, the student expressed frustrations he experienced in his language class because he came

6. A proposed University of Georgia and University of Pennsylvania collaborative project.

into the class with objectives that were completely different from those of his instructor. The instructor's objective was for his students to be able to communicate basically in the language by the end of that first year language course. On the other hand, the student (a linguistics major) was interested in learning the structure of the language so that he could do some analytical work on the language. He was not at all interested in oral proficiency in the language. After weeks of frustration, he said, "I conceded to my teacher's wish so as not to get a 'C' in the class." Is it not possible to have a situation where the curriculum decision is jointly made by both the instructor and the students so that the needs of the student can be put into consideration in curriculum planning?

GBA was proposed to avoid this type of conflict. In a Goal-Based Approach, even though this instructor's objective was not to do a structural analysis of the language in the class, because there was a student whose "need" was to analyze the language, an effort should have been made to provide linguistic terminology in the language to help him do a project in the target language. At the elementary level, the project may be relatively uninvolved. The *task will be tailored to the level of the student*. He or she could be assigned articles to read on the basic structure of the African language even if the article is in English. After all, grammatical notes in foreign language textbooks at the elementary and intermediate levels are usually written in English. If these articles are read in English, the simple task of asking this student to write a one or two page summary of the articles on the structure of that language *in the target language* will be a valuable experience for this student. Using the basic language he or she has learned so far, he or she could also be asked to present his paper to the class in the target language.

As a result, the student is not only learning to communicate and write in the foreign language (the instructor's objective), he or she is also using the language to express issues that address his or her needs (the student's objective). Being able to do this in the foreign language is an added motivation for the student. The result of this situation is that both instructor's and the student's objectives are met without unnecessary conflict. In addition, other students and the instructor listening to this presentation become learners while the student presenter becomes the teacher. Everyone who listens to this student's presentation in class should also benefit from listening to a student using the language to discuss a topic related to his or her academic interest. The presentation could lead to a question and answer session that the instructor will participate in. Every student will be required to do similar projects related to their interests and needs.

Notice that the teacher does not do the research for the student. The student goes to the library to find linguistic articles written about that language in English since at the elementary level the student is not expected to be able to read authentic linguistics journals written in an African language. The role of the instructor is to work with the student to try to express the knowledge he had acquired in English in the African language being studied. In this type of learning environment, both the instructors and the students are learning together.

Notice that at the elementary level, students could read disciplinary texts in English, but they cannot discuss or write their projects in English. The writing and the discussion have to be in the foreign language. The implication of this is that the students as a community of learners have to work together a lot outside of class. Fast learners will be paired with slow learners to work together on their respective projects outside of class before the class presentation. In addition, the instructor will also be available to direct attention to various resources available to help students in their projects. The instructor will also be willing to serve as a resource person. The instructor must model comfortable behavior and establish an atmosphere of learning together. Little and Sanders suggest that "communication does not actually take place in the classroom unless the language learners are a community" (1989, 277).

Searle (1987) has stated that "intent," or the desire to use language for a personal purpose, is the driving force behind all language use. This real-world connection "that immerses students in real communication situations" (Froese 1991, vii) is shared by the proficiency-oriented movement in foreign language teaching (Omaggio-Hadley 1986) and GBA. GBA focuses on language acquisition but encourages the students to use the language to discuss and write topics related to their disciplines, academic, and non-academic interests.

Another important feature of GBA is that, in this approach, the instructors try to shift the responsibility for learning so that it rests more heavily on the students. Notice that underlying this second feature of GBA is the issue of "learner self-management" (Brecht and Walton 1995). GBA emphasizes the importance of self-managed instruction as opposed to "other-managed instruc-tion" for various reasons: (1) learners alone know why they enroll in the course and what they hope to use the language for beyond the classroom situation; (2) learners alone know how best they learn and what can impede their learning; (3) learners who are serious with their learning know that learning is a life-long process, hence their goal is to learn how to manage their own learning. They know that no one can really teach them to speak Hausa, Swahili, or Yoruba. They have to learn to customize their own language learning.

For these reasons, in GBA, learners are allowed to play a major role in what is learned and how it is learned. This does not imply that the instructor loses control over transactions in the classroom. In reality, the instructor (see Brecht and Walton 1995) assumes greater responsibility as a facilitator to make sure that both general educational language objectives and students' goals, needs, and interests for language learning are achieved. The instructor's role is to help the students to see the connection between their language learning and the world beyond school years as pointed out by Brecht and Walton (1995). By "world beyond school years," Brecht and Walton refer to communication tasks that learners intend to achieve with language in real life situations. Such tasks could range from academic (e.g., reading literature in the foreign language, conducting research) to non-academic (e.g., building a relationship or going on a vacation).

The learner-centered approach is central to both GBA and the proficiency-based approach, not only in the teacher-student interactions, but also in the student-student interactions. The teacher delegates the responsibility of helping students to the other students, encourages spontaneous questions, and is a member of the group, but not necessarily the dominant member. The responsibility of the discussion falls on the learners. Similar to the proficiency oriented approach, GBA also emphasizes active, interactive, learning that requires students to work collaboratively to solve problems, complete projects, and complete a task. Through the use of strategies such as cooperative learning, group work, and pair work, students learn to work together, a process resulting in interdependence. As students share their ideas and work, an appreciation for the other individuals will evolve. By making use of all skills (reading, writing, speaking, and listening) all learning styles will be addressed, and the individual learner will have equal access to capitalize on his or her strengths. As the learners learn how to become a life-long learner, they also learn how to work with others in a collaborative manner. Both skills are needed to survive in the real world.

Aside from the learning that goes on in the classroom, the students are also required to find out what is available in the language that relates to their interests and needs. At the elementary level, over the course of the academic term, each student is required to work with metalanguage books, dictionaries, friends who are native speakers, or the instructor on how to express the new knowledge acquired through research in the language of study. The instructor provides the students with simple terms needed to discuss the new information in their own words using the African language they are learning. It is the instructor's responsibility to know how to tailor the task to suit the level and needs of the learner.

Since all of the students are learning new information in their areas of interest and how to express this new information in their new language and culture, the problem with motivation is most likely reduced. Learners are more likely to be more motivated when what they are learning is related to their needs, interests, and goals beyond the school years.

4. HOW GBA WORKS

Even though GBA is applicable to any foreign language, an illustration of how it works with specific examples from a group of Yoruba learners will be given below. On the first day of class, students, (graduate or undergraduate) will be presented with the following questions:

a. What is your major?
b. Why are you learning Yoruba?

Learners usually list majors such as anthropology, literature, art history, history, political science, linguistics, religion, cultural studies, public health, comparative literatures, etc. Asked why they are learning Yoruba, responses usually include:

- the desire to learn about Yoruba religion and the need to use the language in Yoruba religious practices;
- a desire to learn about Yoruba traditional healing practices and the need to be able to address some of these issues in Yoruba;
- the desire to go to Nigeria to do research on Yoruba history and the need to interview local people in Yoruba;
- the need to compare literary works written in Yoruba by Yoruba speakers with works written in English by Yoruba speakers;
- the need to identify some cultural information in Yoruba literary works written in English by Yoruba writers;
- the need to compare some Yoruba cultural aspects with American cultural practices;
- the desire to learn about Yoruba traditional politics and compare it with other traditional West African governing systems;
- the need to discuss the role of Yoruba women in traditional and non-traditional settings;
- the need to use the language to converse with a spouse who is Yoruba;
- the need to spend some time in a Yoruba-speaking area.

Having identified their majors and needs for taking Yoruba, the first-year course began by exposing the students to the language and a variety of functions that can be performed with the language ranging from listening, speaking, writing, and reading very basic authentic texts in the language, using communicative/functional approach to language instruction. Tasks performed are tailored to the level, interests, and needs of each student.

In order to help the students see the relationship between language study and their real-life interests, needs, and motivations for taking the course, the elementary students are all assigned projects related to their needs. This project is usually a semester long and constitutes a major part of the final grade for the course. An elementary student whose major and needs are related to Yoruba history on one hand and West African history on the other will be asked to go to the library to look for an article (in English) on Yoruba History. As mentioned above, the reason why he or she is asked to do the reading in English at this level is because at this level the student cannot read an advanced authentic text on Yoruba history. As pointed out earlier, most of these students study Yoruba for only two years and may not have the opportunity to study the language up to the advanced level, therefore waiting until the time when this student can read authentic Yoruba history texts may not be to the advantage of the student.

The student is allowed to choose any aspect of Yoruba history he or she wants to study in the library. One student chose to do his research on "A Short History on Muslim Religious Practices in Yorubaland." After reading the necessary articles on this topic, his basic task was to try to give a presentation on as simply as possible in the level of language he had acquired so far. He was not expected to give a presentation at the level of a third-year Yoruba student. He was also required to write a page or two on that topic in Yoruba before the presentation. The instructor or a native speaker worked with him to help with some new terminology. He is encouraged to stick to the basic forms of the language that he has learned at that level to make his writing easy and simple. He could read the paper or he could try off memory to tell the class what he has learned on that topic. He was allowed the choice at this basic level. At the end of his short five-minute presentation, other students in the class will ask him few questions on his presentation. The instructor could also ask him questions.

Notice that the instructor is not the one providing this subject matter knowledge base on history to the student. The student, based on his interest and needs researched the topic and came back to the class to give a presentation in Yoruba. There are different levels of learning that is going on here. The history student who did the research, even though it was in English, is acquiring some subject matter knowledge. He works with his instructor, the dictionary, a metalanguage book, or a native speaker to find out how to express some new terms he encountered in his research in Yoruba. It is the instructor's role to help the student learn to keep to the basic structure of the language that he knows in his writing or presentation. But he will be provided with the new terms he needs for his presentation. Before he begins his presentation, he writes the new terms he has learned on the board in Yoruba for other students so that they can follow his presentation. As a result, the other students are learning new Yoruba vocabulary from this student. Notice that the instructor does not have to be an expert in Yoruba history because the instructor and the students are now co-learners on this topic.

This history student is not only learning how to perform

basic functions in Yoruba, he is also learning to express (in Yoruba) some of the Yoruba historical knowledge that he has acquired. By the end of first-year Yoruba, he has not only acquired basic vocabulary but also vocabulary that relates to his needs, interests, and motivations for learning the language. He is required to do at least two such projects by the end of his first year. More highly motivated students often choose to do more than two projects. Even if this student leaves the Yoruba class at the end of first year, he has already acquired the "meta-learning" knowledge (Brecht and Walton 1995, 122) to help him to continue to self-manage his own learning of the language beyond the school years.

At the second-year level, this student is already reading some simple-to intermediate-level authentic texts in Yoruba and his production level is now better than when he was in the elementary course. Apart from the general educational Yoruba language objectives that all the students in the class are attempting to achieve, this history student continues his own research on the history and culture of the language. His paper might now be as long as four to five pages and his in-class presentation may be up to ten minutes. Other students also participate in the learning process by asking questions during the discussion session. The instructor helps to go through different drafts of the written versions of the project before the final draft is submitted. The assessment of the student is not based only on what he has achieved in class but also what he has achieved on his own in relation to his needs. He is also required to do two or more of such projects depending on his interest before the end of the intermediate level. Since most African language learners graduate after the intermediate level, students in this program tend to continue studying Yoruba on their own after leaving the educational system.

Since 1993, students who choose to continue to the advanced level have the opportunity to participate in an Advanced Fulbright-Hays Yoruba Group Project Abroad (USDE-funded) where students spend seven to eight weeks in a Yoruba-speaking area in Nigeria. During this program, participants continue to work on different aspects of Yoruba related to their needs and interests. They are also given the opportunity to use the language they have learned in real life situations. At this level, they can now begin to read difficult authentic texts related to their needs, interests, goals, and motivations. They can also discuss more veried topics with native speakers. Research projects and daily journals in the language are a regular part of this Group Project Abroad.

In the course of three years (1993-1995), and by the end of the advanced level, one Yoruba student interested in History had written and given presentations in Yoruba on topics such as:

a.   *Ogboni* (Secret Cult in Yorubaland).
b.   *Ife ati Oyo ni Itan Awon Eniyan Yoruba* (Ife and Oyo towns in the history of the Yoruba people).
c.   *Ile-Ife: Ilu Pelu Orisiris Asiri* (Ife: a town with a lot of secrets). (Ife is the traditional home land of the Yoruba.)
d.   *Idasile Ilu Ile Ife* (the founding of Ife).
e.   *Itan Soki ti Esin ati Asa Musulumi n'ile Yoruba* (A short history of Muslim religion and practices in Yoruba land).

These are only research topics related to this student's interests and motivations for studying the language. This student happens to be a graduate student. In the same class there were under-graduate students whose interests and needs were based on the different cultural aspects of the language. Such students were encouraged to choose any cultural topic they are interested in and research on this topic in exactly the same way as the history student. Students interested in the literary aspects of the language will also step by step do what the history student did. At the elementary level, they look for topics related to Yoruba literature or of West Africa in general and start writing short essays on the topic until they can write more in the language. They also begin with very short presentations until they get to a stage where they can give a longer presentation.

Some students interested in literature wrote and presented on topics such as:

- *Idagba Iwe-Itan ni ede Yoruba ati Ede Oyinbo ninu ile Yoruba*
- *Amos Tutuola ati D. O. Fagunwa* (Development of Novel Writing in Yoruba and in English in Yoruba land, Amos Tutuola and D. O. Fagunwa). A third semester level student compared the works of Amos Tutuola (a Yoruba writer who writes in English) and D. O. Fagunwa (a Yoruba writer who writes in Yoruba).
- *Ekun Iyawo* (The Songs of the Bride-to-be [Advanced student])
- *Ede Ninu Fiimu Afrika* (Use of Language in African Films). A fourth semester student wrote on why she feels the use of language is not as crucial as the cultural images that people watch in African films.
- *Ede Yoruba Ninu Iwe Henry Loius Gates* (Use of Yoruba language in Henry Loius Gates book *The Signifying Monkey*). This project was done at the end of first Year Yoruba by the same student who wrote on the use of language in African Films.
- *Esin Umbanda ati Candomble* (The Candomble and Umbanda Religion in Brazil).

This paper was written and orally presented by an elementary level Yoruba student who is interested in the survival of Yoruba Religion in the New World. At the intermediate level, this student chose to continue his research on the same topic because it was what he was interested in. By the intermediate level, he covered aspects of that topic that he could not cover at the elementary level.

Some of these topics are published in a book edited by one of the Yoruba students (Jones forthcoming). In all of these projects, the students played a major role in the topics chosen, in *what* they were learning, and in *how* they were learning. The instructor was there to facilitate the learning. The instructor was not expected to be a history, literature, religion, political science specialist. But apart from what was being learned in the class, he or she could guide the students to research topics related to their needs and interests. Since the students for the most part already knew what their interests were, and they knew how to use the library to find some of these information for other subject matter courses, they made use of this research knowledge and applied it to what they were learning in their language class. The instructor continued to let the students see the relationship between their language studies and other subject matter courses they were taking. In the same class, the level of achievements and what is achieved will vary depending on the individual student's interest.

A common question often asked is "How can one instructor cater to the different needs, goals, and interests of one class assuming, for example, that he or she has about 15-20 students in the class?" We should not forget that in this type of self-managed learning (even though it is still partly managed by the instructor; i.e., partly "other-managed" [Brecht and Walton 1995]), the onus is on the learner to achieve his or her learning goals and interests. In addition, why is it possible for a seminar instructor to attend to the varieties of projects that come out of one topic in a seminar class yet it is not possible for a language instructor to attend to similar varieties of students' interests? For example, during one semester, Folarin-Schleicher taught an African linguistics course on "The Structure of African Languages" to about ten under-graduate and graduates students. All the students, with different African language backgrounds, listened to the same lectures and participated in the discussions, activities, and quizzes. At the end of the course, each student, whether graduate or under-graduate, was required to do a project based on the structure of an African language that they spoke or had learned. In this class, there were students of Hausa, Swahili, Arabic, Lingala, Wolof, and Yoruba and each came up with a different linguistic topic related to the structure of the language of interest. Folarin-Schleicher is not an authority in all of these African languages, but as a trained linguist she was able to tailor the topics in this class to accommodate the needs and interests of all these students. Why is this approach not possible in a language course?

The success of GBA, as evidenced in the book published by participating students, shows that it is possible to integrate students' needs, interests, goals, and motivations into the language curriculum as early as the first semester. The level of motivation is also shown in the fact that some of these students were willing to work on the book long after they stopped taking Yoruba. Almost all of the students in this program are aware of the fact that they have to work very hard both inside and outside of the class, but they later appreciate what they could do on their own with the language. One student remarked that "the course provides truly substantive information and requires a great deal of work." Another said that "this class is a motivator. It is definitely a tough class in the respect that a great deal of work is involved both in and outside of class. But again, this reinforces confidence in the language and increases proficiency." In regard to the approach, one student wrote, "the instructor has an unusual and innovative approach to teaching a language class; which is *very* effective. Of the four languages I've studied, this has been the one where I've learned the most the fastest." Some of the students also chose to continue to meet on a regular basis to practice speaking the language even though they were no longer taking the class. This shows that this approach seems to motivate students to want to do more with the language.

A comparison of different projects done by the same student from elementary level to the advanced level and the progress noticed from one level to the other add to the motivation of the student involved. Student evaluations confirm their recognition of the advantages of the approach. They particularly appreciate the fact that they can discuss ideas and issues of substance using their foreign language. Their language class is not just a language class. As one student wrote, "African 373 is more than just a language class, it is a culture class as well. The demands made on me this semester have caused me to put into practical use that which I have learned."

It is important to note that none of the CBI or similar programs includes a single African language. The situation in African language instruction in the U.S. does not permit the luxury of these extra courses where the use of an African language is encouraged outside of African language programs. A brief survey of the status of African language instruction in the U.S. (next chapter) provides an overview of the situation in African language programs.

5. CONCLUSION

This chapter illustrates one way whereby students' needs, goals, interests, and motivations for taking a language course can be integrated into the language educational objectives right from the beginning of the course. This approach is especially valuable for African language programs, most of whose students leave the program after one or two years of language study. It is also beneficial for programs that could not financially afford to have two concurrent classes or groups in order to accommodate students' needs into the language objectives. With GBA, instructors can facilitate self-managed learning, bringing students to see language learning as a lifelong process, teaching them how to learn and how to use their language learning skills to perform communication tasks (based on their needs) well beyond the school years.

GBA shares the objectives of some CBI and LAC programs but differs in the sense that it is a combination of a foreign-language-enriched program and a subject-matter-enriched program. Students are motivated to use the language to perform tasks that relate to their needs and interests. They acquire new information in these areas and are encouraged to express their needs regarding the foreign languages they are learning. Another major difference between GBA and some CBI/LAC programs is that students do not have to have any specific reading ability in the foreign language to participate in this program. As a result, they don't have to be advanced learners of the language before their research, other disciplinary interests, or non-academic interests can be incorporated into the language programs. This also separates GBA from other existing African language programs. As the survey in chapter two indicates, about 27% of

African language instructors showed that they incorporate students' research needs into their language programs at the advanced level. The claim of GBA is that you do not have to wait until the advanced level before this is done; otherwise, most students will leave the program without their needs being fully met since only a handful of students study African languages up to the advanced level.

GBA seems to be one way to implement the theory of Self-Managed Learning (SML) as espoused in Brecht and Walton (1995) even though the GBA program at the University of Wisconsin-Madison began in the fall of 1990. Both GBA and SML share the view that students should be given the responsibility to manage their own learning and language learning careers. They also assume that language programs must focus on program goals and how to meet the needs, motivations, interests, goals, and expectations of their students. Both approaches encourage instructors to play the role of a facilitator who makes curricular decisions in relation to students' interests, needs, and motivations. Nevertheless, contrary to SML, GBA holds to the assumption that, basic language courses can still be both "self-managed" and "other-managed" as demonstrated above, regardless of the student's experience and knowledge. In fact, all the levels—basic, intermediate, and advanced—should be both self-managed and other-managed except that the role of the instructor (other-managed) reduces gradually as you move from the basic level to the advanced level.

The overall goal of this approach is to present a language curriculum that meets the general educational goals and the student's goal for studying the language. The local conditions of African language programs make this approach one way of achieving this overall goal.

CHAPTER SIX

Toward Cultural Proficiency in African Languages

In the last three decades, there has grown a great awareness of Interest in cultural content of the foreign language curriculum. This awareness is reflected in a large body of foreign language literature on the study of target cultures and their relevance to language teaching.[7]

Interest in the communicative and proficiency based approaches to foreign language teaching in the '80s and the '90s has also given the teaching of culture a boost. Galloway (1985) notes that the ability to communicate in another language requires not only knowledge of the grammatical system of a language but also knowledge of the patterns of living, acting, reacting, seeing,

---

7. Brooks 1968 and 1971; Dodge 1972; Nostrand 1974; Seelye 1976 and 1984; Lafayette 1975 and 1978; Allen 1985; Fantini 1997; Folarín-Schleicher 1998.

and explaining the world of the target country as well. Omaggio-Hadley (1993) also states that the teaching of culture as a topic in its own right and as it is embedded in language use is an important aspect of language teaching that is oriented toward communicative proficiency. Therefore, "the study of culture must be integrated with the study of language if students are to derive lasting benefits from their language learning experience" (Omaggio-Hadley 1993, 359).

Culture viewed as an essential part of proficiency in the foreign language was also brought into the limelight by the inclusion of culture in the *ACTFL Provisional Proficiency Guidelines* of 1984.

There is no doubt that it is not easy to teach culture since it is very fluid and it encompasses various disciplines. Crawford-Lange and Lange (1984) also pointed out that one of the problems with teaching culture in foreign language classrooms is that many language teachers feel that their knowledge of the target language is inadequate because of the limited exposure they have had to the culture. In addition, familiarity with culture does not imply the ability to integrate the teaching of that culture into language teaching. Because of these reasons, culture poses a strong challenge to many foreign language teachers.

1. THE CURRENT STATUS OF CULTURE IN AFRICAN LANGUAGE TEXTBOOKS

A cursory look at some of the most widely used textbooks for Hausa, Swahili, and Yoruba shows that the teaching of culture in our African language classrooms, especially at the elementary level, is sporadic and peripheral. The cultural content of our textbooks is limited and overshadowed by a strong emphasis in grammatical analysis. The argument has been that our students can acquire the necessary cultural knowledge by taking courses in anthropology, other African studies programs, or by traveling to the country where the African language is spoken. In most cases we assume that our students are in African Studies and, they will, therefore, get sufficient exposure to African culture outside the language classroom. Some of us also expect our students to gain cultural knowledge as they master the grammatical points/forms of the language.

While it is true that some of our students do major in African Studies, there are, however, some whose only exposure to African culture is through their study of the language. Arasanyin, et al. (1998) noted in their survey that about 70% of our students are undergraduates who do not necessarily major in African Studies. In addition, there are some aspects of African cultures that cannot be fully understood except through the language. For example, the use of the various forms of address and polite expressions in Yoruba can be fully appreciated in a Yoruba class. Given the substantial differences between Western and African cultures when compared with the similarities between American and European cultures, the addition of the cultural component in the African language curriculum makes a significant contribution to the overall development of our students' proficiency in the language.

Using the evaluation framework developed by Pfister and Borzilleri (1977), we will attempt to evaluate several kinds of cultural information and the manner in which this information has been presented in first-year African language textbooks from 1904-1998. Some modification of the design was done as it applies to African languages. We will also take into consideration the cultural goals set by Lafayette (1978) as a broad framework within which cultural objectives can be defined for African languages. The evaluation was done for first-year textbooks in Bambara, Chichewa, Fula, Hausa, Igbo, Kanuri, Kikuyu, Kirundi, Lingala, Luganda, Ndebele, Sango, Shona, Swahili, Wolof, Xhosa, Yoruba, and Zulu. These are the most common African languages for which first-year textbooks are available.

In order to determine whether a particular African language textbook is adequate or not (in terms of its cultural content and presentation), we will try to answer the following questions:

1. How does the text present traditional family organization and the personal sphere along the lines of (Hall 1959), including the nuclear and extended family, family institutions, and rights of passage (birth, naming, initiation, marriage, and death)?
2. How does the text present the social organization of the culture apart from family organization?
3. Are traditional African political systems and institutions presented (e.g., religion and cosmology, the interpretation of everyday events, economic-occupational, marriage, educational, etc.)?
4. How does the text present the operation of public institutions such as health care, transportation, and education?
5. Are African the arts and aesthetics presented (e.g., African oral tradition, literature music, dance, clothing, graphic arts etc.)?
6. Are active and passive everyday cultural patterns presented to reflect the essence of everyday life?
7. Are cultural materials presented in a sequence to aid in the familiarity and simplicity of the language?
8. Are cultural materials distributed throughout the textbook?

9. Is the cultural diversity of our students taken into consideration in presenting the cultural materials? (In most cases many nationalities, are represented in the class).
10. Do the texts and dialogues represent *authentic* situations?
11. Is culture presented to reflect the essence of everyday life?
12. How does the text present matters of politeness and etiquette? Are contrasts between African and western concepts of acceptable and unacceptable behavior shown?
13. In each of these topics, how does the text treat the contrasts and conflicts between traditional cultures and the imposition of Western culture?
14. Are questions for content and cultural understanding presented at the end of the reading?
15. Is the textbook acceptable?

Only three textbooks (Table 6.1) include information about the family unit and personal relationships, the social sphere, and political systems and institutions (items 1-3). These account for many of the textbooks identified in chapter one as audio-lingual texts. Most do not identify dialogue participants as Africans and most dialogues are presented as conversations between "A" and "B" or "teacher" and "student." Dialogues mostly teach grammatical structures. Some do not describe participants; others give questions and answers with no speakers indicated. Most textbooks are full of phonological drills, grammar drills, patterned drills. It is hard to identify any cultural contexts in most of the dialogues. One can hardly tell how people live from day to day. There is no information about occupations, religion, education in the traditional African culture, physical resources, travel and transportation, literature, music, architecture, geography, clothing, adornment, cuisine, or other African cultural detail.

Items	Yes	No	Adequate	Inadequate
1. Family/personal sphere	3	31	2	32
2. Social organization	3	31	2	32
3. Political systems and institutions	3	31	2	32
4. Public institutions	1	33	1	33
5. Arts and aesthetics	1	33	1	33
6. Active and passive cultural forms	3	31	2	32
7. Culture in sequence	2	32	2	32
8. Cultural information distribution	2	32	2	32
9. Cultural diversity of students	1	33	1	33
10. Texts and dialogues in authentic situations	2	32	2	32
11. Culture presents everyday life	1	33	1	33
12. Politeness and etiquette	3	31	2	32
13. Traditional and Western cultures	2	32	2	32
14. Questions for cultural understanding	1	33	1	33
15. Is the textbook acceptable?			**1**	**33**

Table 6.1. Evaluation of the cultural information in self-contained African language textbooks published 1965-1998.

Very few of the textbooks that have cultural notes have any on greetings or forms of address. Little else is said about the culture. In addition, there are usually no exercises that follow the few cultural notes in the textbooks. This is in contrast to grammatical notes that are followed by many grammar exercises.

At the expense of emphasizing grammatical information, some of the dialogues in most of the textbooks are culturally inappropriate. Examples were found in some languages where honorific pronouns are used for adults but the dialogue shows participants addressing others first by name and then continuing with conversation using honorific pronouns for the referent. It was culturally inappropriate to alternate the use of an honorific pronoun and the first name of that same addressee. The use of honorific pronouns in some African languages implies that the addressee is older. Because status is linked to age, it is culturally inappropriate to use first names in a case as described above. The same status and respect is the same regardless of gender which means that constructed dialogues between a mother and a child would observe the same rules.

Two books were found that adequately distributed, cultural information that was well sequenced to facilitate comprehension without unnecessary linguistic complications. We also found that at least one contrastive and/or similar cultural aspect was taken up in each chapter either in some dialogue and/or specific cultural reading exercise or text extracted from authentic situations. There was considerable effort, in two books, to show perceived conflicts between traditional African culture and Western culture.

Of the thirty-four first-year, self-contained African language textbooks published between 1904 and 1998, only one can be considered culturally adequate based on the 1-15 items in Table

6.1. This particular book presents the various cultural information necessary to portray everyday life of the speakers of the target language. It is the only book that incorporates questions, exercises, and tasks that encourage the students to compare and contrast their culture of the target language.

These questions test content understanding and cultural understanding. The questions usually take the cultural diversity of the learners into consideration. In other words, learners are encouraged to talk about their own relevant experiences concerning the cultural topic discussed. This comparison is clearly missing in the other textbooks that have culture notes and questions.

For a textbook to be culturally acceptable, it must not only present information from items one to 15; It must also adequately direct students' attention to cultural differences and similarities. Unless questions are directed to compare African cultures with the students' cultures, students will neither gain a greater perspective on their own cultures nor a greater understanding of themselves as individuals from a particular culture.

If cultural information is so poorly presented in most of our African language first-year textbooks, the immediate concern will be to develop a cultural curriculum that could guide African language textbook writers to prepare texts that will overtly present cultural information and integrate these information into the language learning activities. This task is especially crucial for the field of African language pedagogy because the majority of African language teachers are in fields other than second language acquisition. Up until now, in the United States only the University of Wisconsin, Madison offers a course on methods of teaching African languages. Most instructors learn to teach the language on the job. As noted in chapter two, the most common training in African language instruction is characterized by two or five days of workshop given to incoming teaching assistants to prepare them for teaching their respective African languages.

As a result, the majority of instructors rely heavily on textbooks to determine their curricula. It is sometimes possible to find some experienced teachers who have learned to use textbooks as an accessories. However, most of teachers of African languages in the U.S.—particularly teaching assistants or lecturers who (in most cases) are not fully committed to the teaching of the language—do not use textbooks as accessories but rather as teaching tools. It is understandable they would elect to do so. Many are underpaid and often accept positions for lack of better opportunities. Others are graduate students pursuing full-time program of study in their own disciplines, and teaching African languages serves as a part-time job on short- term basis. Thus, the time they would want to devote to teaching and exploring teaching materials is limited, resorting to a textbook as the only readily available resource for accomplishing their teaching objectives. A comprehensive textbook with adequate cultural material would be more useful for such teachers.

Before showing how cultural information can be integrated into our grammar-based textbooks, it is important to determine what our cultural objectives or goals will be.

2. DETERMINING OUR CULTURAL GOALS

One of the most important aspects of incorporating cultural information into our language curriculum is that we make it a carefully planned and integral component. The following goals are offered as useful starting points, as resources for the development of a local set of goals that will reflect the priorities of each language program.

Seelye (1984) and Lafeyette (1988) proposed a number of goals that can be adapted to African languages. Some can serve as a working base from which to determine our own cultural goals. In what follows, we will present some of Lafayette's goals and illustrate how they can apply to different African cultures. The student will be able to:

1. Recognize/explain major geographical monuments (e.g., recognizing different countries where Hausa is spoken, major cities in Hausaland, weather patterns, information about number of Hausa speakers, etc.);
2. Recognize/explain major historical events pertaining to a particular group of Africans (e.g., the different phases of the history of the Swahili people, the impact of colonization on the Swahili people and culture, the effect of slavery on different African languages and cultures, etc.);
3. Recognize/explain major administrative, political, religious, educational institutions (e.g., understanding traditional and modern political structures imposed on Africans, the impact of traditional religion on Christianity and Islam and vice versa, conflicts between traditional African values and modern Western values, etc.);
4. Recognize/explain major aesthetic achievements of African cultures from architecture, literature, oral tradition, and the arts (e.g., becoming acquainted with Yoruba oral traditions and literary genres, their clothing, their notion of "beauty," traditional Yoruba music, etc.);
5. Recognize/explain "active" everyday cultural patterns such as eating, shopping, greeting people, entertaining, playing

sports, etc., (e.g., knowing that younger people do not initiate greetings with *"Bawo ni?"* to an adult, being acquainted with the Bagandas' (Luganda speakers) ways of buying and selling, knowing what Chichewa speakers do to entertain themselves, etc.);

6. Recognize/explain passive everyday cultural patterns such as social stratification, marriage, work, etc. (e.g., what kinds of ceremonies the Lingala speakers do for naming ceremonies, weddings, house warming; the major traditional occupations of the Igbo people, how these jobs conflict with modern occupations, etc.);

7. Act appropriately in common everyday situations (e.g., knowing that it means a lot to an African for you to eat with them when they offer you food; using the "honorific" pronoun when addressing an adult in Yorubaland as a sign of respect; not offering to shake hands with adults in Yorubaland unless the adult initiates the handshaking; understanding that Hausa men prefer not to shake hands with women, etc.);

8. Use appropriate common gestures (e.g., knowing that the Yoruba girls kneel down to greet an adult while the boys prostrate themselves, that the Hausas squat to greet one another, that the gestures that go with "yes" and "no" in some African cultures may be opposite form those in your culture, etc.);

9. Value and appreciate different peoples and societies (e.g., understand that Africans are no less human than other peoples in the world, develop empathy for their ways of life even they are different from yours, identify similarities in your culture and that of the Shona culture, for example, without concentrating on the differences between your culture and the particular African culture, etc.);

123

10. Evaluate the validity of statements about African cultures (e.g., all Africans keep "African time," all African women play a subordinate role in all African societies, all African cultures are the same, etc.) .

It is important to know that each of the goals stated above can be integrated into our first-year African language curriculum. We do not need to wait until the second-year or the third-year levels before we begin to incorporate this cultural information into our language curriculum. As pointed out in chapter 2, for the majority of our students, the first-year level may be the only level of language instruction they will take because most of our students come into African language classes after they have taken some years of a European language in high school. It is, therefore, crucial that we incorporate this cultural information as effectively as possible in our first-year language curriculum.

Having decided on our cultural objectives, the next task is to show how these objectives can be incorporated into our language textbooks.

2. INTEGRATING CULTURE INTO LANGUAGE MATERIALS

In order, to develop a culturally rich textbook, one might simply divide the material up into themes, vocabulary, and grammar and match it to the cultural topics. As Allen (1988) pointed out, by doing this one will be teaching or presenting the language through the culture of its speakers rather than teaching culture through language. She refers to the approach (teaching culture through the language) as the "main meal-dessert" approach where students only have access to the cultural information after they have digested the grammar. She suggested that for each lesson in the textbook, we should identify at least one cultural concept that would serve as the point of departure for the presentation of each isolated grammar point.

2.1 An Example of a Culture-Based Materials Presentation

In the following presentation, we will use Yoruba, a language spoken in Nigeria, Benin, and Togo.

Lesson Objectives/Goals

Topic: Clothing
Function: Talking about different kinds of clothes in Yoruba-
           land, describing how people dress and what they
           wear
Grammar: Finding different ways of saying "to wear/ to put
           on" in Yoruba, the conditional maker, use of
           interrogative adjectives such as "what type of—?"

Cultural Information: Formal versus informal dress in
           Yorubaland.

SECTION ONE
Begin the lesson by presenting a list of vocabulary dealing with different kinds of clothes in Yorubaland. Each item would be

illustrated to show the learner what it looks like. For example:

Aṣọ Obìnrin (women's clothes)

Gèlè	head gear
bùba	loose blouse
ìró	wrapper
ìboorùn	shawl

Aṣọ Ọkùnrin (men's clothes)

fìlà	cap
ṣòkòtò	loose pants
bùbá	loose long robe
agbádá	flowing robe

Aṣọ Òyìnbó (European clothes)

kaba	dress
búláósì	blouse
àgbékọ́	slip
súwẹ̀tà	sweater
síkááfù	scarf

Activities for Section One (these would be done in the target language)

- Point at a piece of cloth and ask your partner what the cloth is called in Yoruba.
- Show your partner a picture of different kinds of people and ask him or her to tell you what those people wear.

SECTION TWO
Present a monologue of a Yoruba man or woman talking about a particular occasion he or she attended and what was worn for that occasion.

Activities for the Monologue
- Ask questions to show that the students understand the content.
- Ask the students what they would wear if they were going to a similar occasion.

SECTION THREE
Present grammar information to show how to ask questions such as:

- What did you wear to the party yesterday? (In Yoruba we can use "What kind of cloth did you wear?")

Present grammar information about the different ways of saying "to put on —" in Yoruba.

Grammar Activities
- Ask questions that would show that the students can use the question form "What kind of ____ ?"
- Ask questions that would show that the students can use the different forms of the verb "to put on" in Yoruba.

SECTION FOUR: CULTURAL INFORMATION
Present cultural information on the type of clothes that are culturally appropriate for the Yoruba people and those that are not.

- How do the Yoruba people dress for a formal and non-formal occasion? Are there proverbs in Yoruba that illustrate the importance of clothing among the Yorubas?—If there are, mention some and explain what they mean.
- What kinds of clothes will be offensive to a traditional Yoruba person?
- Can Yoruba men wear what is traditionally regarded as women's clothes and vice versa?

For a first-year textbook, the note should be as simple and authentic as possible. All of this information could be presented through cultural notes, a video presentation which is a companion to the textbook, role-plays presented in a form of a dialogue, or any other form appropriate for a first year level.

Cultural activities

- Ask students questions that would show that they understand the content of the cultural text.
- Ask students questions that would help them to compare and contrast the cultural information they have learned to their own culture.
- Ask students to role play a situation where they would select some clothes for a particular occasion in Yorubaland. Ask why they would select those particular clothes.
- Ask students what they would wear for different occasions in their culture and whether women can wear what is traditionally regarded as men's clothing in their culture?
- Show students some pictures of Yoruba men and women and ask them to predict the type of place they would go dressed in that type of attire.

SECTION FIVE

Present a dialogue between two people illustrating a conversation about clothing. For example, there could be a dialogue between two friends in which one is planning to attend an important event and asks for suggestions from another friend concerning what to wear and what it is affordable. Show pictures of two people who are engaged in the dialogue.

Dialogue activities

- Ask questions that show whether they understand the dialogue or not.
- Ask questions to identify any cultural information from the dialogue
- Ask questions that would help the students to relate the information from the dialogue to their own situations.
- Ask students to play the roles of the two people in the dialogue but applying the context to their own situations.

SECTION SIX

Any authentic text on clothing could be presented in this section. Text should also be followed by questions that test content and cultural understanding.

The sample lesson above illustrates a "multidimensional curriculum" (see Stern 1983) whereby linguistic, cultural, communicative, and general education information are all integrated within each lesson. This kind of curriculum stresses the learning of both the content (culture) and form (grammar and vocabulary). By presenting language through culture, our students can have true communicative competency in the target African language.

4. DIFFERENT WAYS OF TEACHING CULTURES

Many strategies have been proposed for integrating culture into classroom activities. Some of these strategies are Culture Capsule (Taylor and Sorensen 1961, Seelye 1984), the Culture Cluster (Meade and Morain, 1973), the Culture Assimilator (Fiedler, Mitchell, and Triandis 1971), Culture Mini-dramas (Seelye 1984), the Micrologue, the Audio-Motor Unit (see Allen 1985 and Ommagio-Hadley 1993, for other strategies). Some of these strategies primarily convey information about the target culture while others encourage process strategies on the parts of the students.

4.1 Six Instructional Goals for Teaching Culture Based Communicative Competence

Following from Nostrand's (1970) culturally relevant skills that can be developed in the classroom, Seelye (1993) proposed six instructional goals upon which teachers can base their classroom instruction. Outlined below are goals that illustrate how a foreign language teacher can approach the task of developing learners' skill in the socially contextual areas necessary for intercultural communicative competence:

• Goal 1—Interest: The student shows curiosity about another culture (or another segment or subculture of one's own culture) and empathy toward its members.
• Goal 2—Who: The student recognizes that role expectations

and other social variables such as age, sex, social class, religion, ethnicity, and place of residence affect the ways people speak and behave.

- Goal 3—What: The student realizes that effective communication requires discovering the culturally conditioned images that are evoked in the minds of people when they think, act, and react to the world around them.
- Goal 4—Where and When: The student recognizes that situational variables and conventions shape behavior in important ways.
- Goal 5—Why: The student understands that people generally act the way they do because they are using options their society allows for satisfying basic physical or psychological needs and that cultural patterns are interrelated and tend to support need/satisfaction mutually.
- Goal 6—Exploration: The student can evaluate a generalization about a given culture in terms of the amount of evidence substantiating it, and has the skills needed to locate and organize information about a culture from the library, the mass media, people, and personal observation.

In other words, we can help students to develop interest in social and cultural roles and motives (goals 1-5). Furthermore, we can help students develop an interest in finding out more about the culture on their own (goal 6).

An obvious question at this point is "How can a topic such as clothing be worked into the framework of these six goals? The example below illustrates how this may be achieved.

TOPIC

Clothing

Goal 1 How much interest do students have in the different Yoruba clothes? Will they be interested in trying some out?

Goal 2 Do women wear the same clothing as men? Do younger people dress similarly to older people? How do the Yoruba chiefs and *Obas* (kings) dress? Are there any differences in the ways married and single women dress? How about older men and women?

Goal 3 What are the different kinds of clothes available to everyone in Yoruba culture? What are they made of? Are they hand-woven or tie-dyed or batik? Are there differences between traditional clothes and modern clothes Yoruba?

Goal 4 What clothes are appropriate for which occasions? Are there differences between formal and informal attires? When can you wear what kind of clothes? During various Yoruba festivals, do people dress differently or do they wear whatever is appropriate for a formal or informal gathering?

Goal 5 What are the Yoruba people's view on clothing? Are there proverbs that illustrate these views? For example, there is a Yoruba proverb that says that *"ìrínisí ni ìsænilôjö"* ("you will be treated the way you appear in public"). What does that say about Yoruba views on clothing? If the Yoruba people believe that "you will be treated the way you appear in public," that could illustrate why Yoruba place important emphasis on appearance, including what they wear. Are there other proverbs or poems that illustrate why the Yoruba people dress the ways they do?

Goal 6 Are there other resources aside from the information given by the teacher through which students can find out more about Yoruba clothing and modes of dress? Are there video tapes that illustrate how people dress for different occasions? If so students can watch them and report their findings to the class. Are there native speakers that students can talk to through email or other media about Yoruba clothing? The students can do a project comparing and contrasting all of the above information in relation to Yoruba clothing with issues related to clothing in their own culture.

Depending on the questions teachers ask, it is possible to relate any cultural theme to as many of the above instructional goals as possible. Teachers can help their students to develop both cultural and linguistic competencies by showing them how to use the language to express the cultural matters outlined above.

5. PROBLEMS WITH TEACHING CULTURE

There are many reasons why African language courses often have no systematic integration of culture. The most common is the notion that students do not have enough language to read or understand cultural materials in the target language; hence there is the temptation to wait until the intermediate or advanced level before introducing authentic cultural materials (see the survey in chapter two). As a result, most first-year African language classes are strongly grammar-based. Many African language instructors believe that it will be easier for students to understand discussions about the culture in the target language *after* they have acquired the language (Galloway 1985a). This approach is referred to as the "main meal-dessert approach" by Allen (1983).

The disadvantage of this approach in African language pedagogy, as we have already explored, is that most African language learners only learn the language for one year (see Arasanyin, et al. 1996). This does not allow much time for African language learners to receive a comprehensive cultural instruction (Seelye 1984). The solution is to find a way to systematically integrate cultural information into the language curriculum, as illustrated in section three. Cultural materials written in the learner's first language could be assigned outside of class while classroom discussions of the materials could remain simple as possible in the target language. The goal, of course, is to maximize the amount of time spent in the classroom using the target language.

Another reason is a lack of adequate training in language pedagogy among African language instructors (see chapter two). Crawford-Lange and Lange (1984) also propose that language teachers may not have been adequately trained in the teaching of culture and, therefore, do not have strategies for integrating cultural studies into language classes or for creating viable frameworks for organizing instruction around cultural themes. Instructors who are native speakers of the language (or non-native speakers who have lived in the target country for a long time) are usually hired to teach African languages because of their knowledge of the language and the culture; however, it is one thing to have the knowledge of a subject, but it is another thing

134

to be able to impart that knowledge to others. Instructors who know both the language and the culture very well—but do not have any pedagogical training or who have had only a few days workshop to prepare them for their teaching—end up teaching the culture of the language in English (where English is the first language of the learners) in the form of a lecture, especially at the first-year level. One excuse for this practice is that it is important for the students to learn about the culture of the people whose language they are learning, but the students will not understand the cultural information if the instructor uses the target language. A language class in this case is turned into a social studies class where the students learn about the target culture in English. This practice of teaching the target culture in a language other than the target language limits the exposure of the students to the target language in the classroom. Research (Krashen 1982) has shown that language learners learn better when they are exposed to the language in a way in which they understand it. It is important that language learners be taught in the target language. Instructors trained well in pedagogy could make this a possibility.

The third major problem with teaching culture in African language classrooms is a common lack of cultural knowledge by the instructors themselves especially if they are not native speakers of the language and have never lived in the target culture. In some cases, the instructors may know the structure of the language very well but lack cultural competency. As a result, they may be nervous and hesitant about teaching culture, just as any teacher might be uneasy about teaching a subject without substantial knowledge of and or training in the subject. The problem with this uneasiness is that the instructor may accord the "uncomfortable" subject a somewhat lower priority in order to avoid dealing with it (Pesola 1991, 344). Even if teachers' knowledge of the culture is limited, it is important for them to know that their role is not to impart facts but "to help students attain the skills that are necessary to make sense out of the facts they themselves discover in their study of the target culture" (Omaggio-Hadley 1993, 358; Seelye 1984).

As in most areas of the curriculum, another effective way for teachers to deal with culture is to consider themselves co-learners, encouraging questions and working together with the students to locate answers.

6. CONCLUSION

As established in the beginning of this chapter, it is critical to recognize that language cannot be separated from the cultural framework in which and *through which* it exists. Culture must, therefore, be an integral part of language learning if the student is to communicate in that language. The integration of culture into our language textbooks is one of the ways we may demonstrate the importance of culture in language acquisition. The textbook, according to Levno and Pfister (1980, 52), is "the primary tool of the foreign language classroom; therefore, it is essential that the tool present the target culture adequately."

In this chapter, we have provided a design for evaluation that is used to access some of the African language textbooks for first year learners. It is intended to provide African language teachers with an easy and objective evaluative measure for the adequacy or inadequacy of a college-level, self-contained, first-year African language textbook. It is meant to serve as a sample design that can be modified according to the needs of the instructor.

The teaching of cultural competency is better achieved when language instruction is presented through the culture as opposed to teaching the structure first before teaching the culture. The problems associated with teaching culture can be better handled with proper pedagogical training and when teachers see themselves not as people who impart facts but as co-learners inquiring about the target culture.

CHAPTER SEVEN

The Use of Audio-Visual and Emerging Technologies

The use of computer-based instructional materials and other low level audio-visual materials in education has one major purpose: to enhance the learning process. Effective uses of pictures, charts, maps, films, videos, or slides requires careful planning. Little is gained by simply showing these cultural artifacts in class. Audio-visual materials provide excellent opportunities for learner-centered instruction and provide a way to encourage students to be creative as well as to engage in critical thinking. They also provide meaningful contexts while they enhance interactive participation. Because students have to be creative in composing ideas, audio-visual materials help them to organize information and put it to use. There are also often intrinsic motivations for the students; they create their own reasons for the information they deduct from the audio and video materials. The ability to watch a video or film and then discuss its content in the target language is part art (creative) and part science (analytic).

1. BACKGROUND

As institutions move to use computers in instruction, teachers in the less commonly taught languages will be forced to adapt in order to compete and retain students who are genuinely interested in learning African languages. The field cannot take cover under the fact that it is a few years behind the commonly taught languages in terms of manpower and resources. Students who come to our classes are not only interested in learning African languages for their linguistic merits, but also to expand their knowledge of the world and its peoples. Thus, they would want to be taught using new modes, methodologies found in other learning environments. Consequently, the twenty-first century African languages field-development agenda has to include computer-based-instruction in its framework.

It is inevitable that although teachers of African languages will be faced with the same problems that faced teachers of other subjects, but they maybe affected by those problems the most. The two immediate problems are space and availability of computers. A survey of institutions show that where computers are available, they are located in general places and are not ubiquitous enough for all of the students in a class. Thus local conditions contribute as factors affecting computers' availability and usefulness for language instruction. For example, while the University of Georgia and University of Wisconsin would be affected by the number of computers available to students space and location at both schools are not issues since both have made provisions for the use of computers for their African languages programs.

The University of Georgia, for example, has a computer lab devoted to the teaching of African languages. Georgia has assigned twenty Power Macs and ten iMac computers and eight PCs for exclusive use in African language instruction. These computers are connected to the university network and share a server maintained by the Department of Comparative Literatures (the home of the language programs). This is a privilege which is not enjoyed by programs at many other schools in the United States. It is also an envious position well beyond the current reach of other African language programs considering the development limitations we discussed in chapter one.

The third problem is the selection of well-designed courseware that meets classroom needs. This problem is significant, considering our discussion of materials development in chapter one. As is the case of text materials, procedures for courseware evaluation, selection, and purchase are not well developed (a problem for all disciplines and not unique to African languages). With commercial competition to develop and sell software, many programs will enjoyed cost-effective products; they may, from time to time, waste a great deal of money buying courseware or software which will turn out to be less useful.

The fourth problem concerns computer literacy. Programs will have to require teachers to be computer-literate in order to make efficient and cost-effective uses of multimedia instructional software and courseware. Considering that program affiliations and institutional structures are germane to program and field development, it raises a lot of questions. Is this viable in the current structures as described? We are expecting the kind of teachers we have in some of the programs around the nation to be computer-competent in language instruction even though their interests do not always reside in this area. We are also demanding that programs hire teachers whose academic backgrounds and career interests are in language instruction. How many programs are ready and willing to do that?

The point here is that the field of African language instruction is being challenged by the forces of change coming with the new millennium. Thus, the use of technology in African language instruction warrants a national debate which examines the support which programs are receiving on college campuses and how much the teaching of African languages is an integral part of the college curriculum.

Having said this, we need to assert that the field is ready and eager to keep up with current trends in technology. Where the climate is right, programs will make major strides in the uses of technology, starting with what is affordable and available. In this chapter, we will explore different possibilities, starting with low level technology, for the use of video on television monitors. We will then look at possibilities for using computers and future developments.

2. USING VIDEO OR FILMS FOR LANGUAGE INSTRUCTION

When people watch an entertainment video, they do so with the intention of enjoying the images, even if they do not understand all of the words spoken. Students should be encouraged to do the same with videos although they will be required to perform some specific tasks to facilitate learning. The outstanding feature of video is that they can represent complete communicative situations. The combination of sound and image is dynamic, immediate, and accessible to the learner; therefore, videos and films from Africa or any other part of the world can be used in class for instructional purposes even though the language used is not the target language (but rather the metalanguage).

The challenge for the teacher is in using the content to stimulate discussions and critical thinking in the classroom using the target language. The teacher's facilitative role should be visible. He or she should take time to discuss the main concepts in the film in a context that fits life in Africa. In a learner-centered mode of instruction, video or film becomes the means through which the learner explores the world. Independent of the teacher, the learner formulates thoughts and ideas and organizes them into coherent discourse chunks that he or she can share with others. In the process of sharing, not only does the learner develop his or her proficiency but also exhibits the student's own artistic and scientific abilities which are not necessarily embodied in language but on the student's general intellectual abilities and critical thinking skills.

When video or film are used well, they can provide students with key structures and vocabulary items which are essential for building their proficiency. It is, therefore, necessary for the teacher to prepare well for the interactive learning process especially when the viewing is done in class. Preparation includes previewing the video to acquaint oneself with the level of language used, major themes, sub-themes, and general information. The teacher then has to make a decision on the best approach viewing the material. An experienced teacher can use a video or film in the target language with students at any level (elementary, intermediate, advanced). For example, at one stage, the teacher can emphasize cultural proficiency rather than language use and proficiency. Language use and proficiency are only valuable if the acquisition process is made real.

In any video, the speakers of the target language can be seen and heard. In some cases, the video can provide contexts which are conducive to valuable cultural and/or social discussions. Issues relating to personal or male-female relationships, parents, kinship relations, and the community are good sources of topics for creative discussions. With the help of a teacher, students can develop ideas for discussion from the images on the screen. For example, the ages of the participants, their genders, perhaps their relationships with one another, social status, and their main activities can fuel discussion. Furthermore, paralinguistic information such as facial expressions or hand gestures is available to accompany aural clues toward various linguistic details which are crucial in maintaining the level of proficiency expected.

3. HELPING STUDENTS TO LEARN FROM VIDEO AND FILM

As noted earlier, successful learning from film or video include careful planning, students' abilities to transfer knowledge from the images and accompanying language, accurate background information brought into the viewing, and information gathering process. Most of all, it must include the teacher's ability to guide students to the proper use of content and context to stimulate an informed discussion.

There are different ways in which the teacher can introduce

film or video materials to learners: (1) showing videos or films with or without sound and (2) using single or repeated viewing. In each case, it is important for the teacher to establish a specific task in which the viewer is engaged. Viewing a portion or an entire episode without an established objective is futile and counterproductive because it limits the learner's ability to move from the viewing stage to the creativity stage. The role of the teacher is critical. The teacher must always take care to harness the power of the video material. As a facilitator, he or she must create a successful viewing environment and provide enough background information to enhance understanding. It is the teacher who has the primary responsibility for creating a successful viewing environment.

Successful use of the video or film presupposes a successful application of certain fundamental pedagogical principles. The challenges are doubled by the mere fact that this requires a combination of skills both on the parts of the teacher and the students. Both have to possess the skill of extracting information from audio-visual material. The teacher has to be able to use the skill *to guide the students to use their skills* to be creative in a context that may appear alien to them. Because the students come to class with skills acquired from watching movies and television on their own, the level of expertise in extracting information from audio material can be very high. The teacher's role is to make sure that the students are not watching the film or video for entertainment purposes only, but to actually learn something new and use it to create something that they can share with their classmates and the world at large. It is critical when African film and video is used to teach about Africa because students may come to class with false beliefs and stereotypes that can make the teacher's job a little harder than normal. The teacher should see this challenge as an opportunity to correct misinformation the students may have about the content and contexts being explored.

Another challenge is the use of authentic language in the film or video. Often, one of the reasons teachers give for not using video or film is that the language level is beyond the students' general proficiency level. What they do not realize is that it is not necessary for students to possess a high proficiency level (in this case native speaker level) before they can be exposed to authentic film and video. Students should not be expected to understand everything said on the film or video. Students are capable of inferring a great deal, even without linguistic expertise. Most importantly the students should be able to re-tell the story in their own words using the tools and resources already acquired. That is why multiple viewings of a film or video, a couple of which should be in mute, are so crucial in teaching language and culture. Experience teaches us that even native speakers of a language would produce different interpretations of the same movie. It is, therefore, unrealistic to emphasize and require accuracy "to the T" of the students' storyline after one or any number of viewing of a film or video.

To assist students in getting the most out of film or video, the teacher should prepare a step-by-step viewing guide, necessary vocabulary items, reporting outline (e.g., fill in the blanks or guided short sentence summaries). The teacher should encourage repeated viewing both in class and as an assignment to enable the students to bring out different aspects of the video or film that enhance both the understanding of the content and context on which the information is based.

This guided structure, whose function is basically reinforcing material learned before and during the viewing stages, need not always be individualized. Better results are obtained if the students are encouraged to work in groups of two or more (but fewer than five) on a specific topic. Activities may include role playing, picture stories, report, and/or critiques of the film. The teacher may assist the students who have trouble identifying specific contexts which appear to be beyond their abilities. However, the teacher should exercise caution against opening the field too wide. The idea is to make this a student-centered approach but at the same time teacher-controlled in order to avoid making students too dependent on the teacher for linguistic and additional kinds of information. In other words, the teacher's involvement should be minimal while the role remains that of facilitator.

3.1 Elementary Level

At the elementary level, for example, a successful video or film class will depend on the lesson plan and not the students' proficiency level. For elementary students, it is necessary that the video be shown twice, regardless of whether the footage uses the target language or not. If the language used is also the target language, at least the first viewing should be in mute. The students should then be instructed on the aspects of culture (which should be the main goal at this level). Sound may be included in subsequent viewing for the purpose of exposing the students to the segmental and supragegmental (sounds, melody, intonation, tone, accent) features of the language. If the video or film contains words or structures which have already been introduced in the class, the teacher can highlight them and ask the students to track them down, identifying the contexts in which they may have been used in the film or video. At the end of the presentation, the instructor can ask the students to perform a variety of tasks such as (1) object naming; (2) listing specific actions performed by those who appeared on the video/film, events which are central to the story or documentary; and (3) selecting specific events and using them to develop simple sentences or dialogues that match the actual event(s) seen.

In (1), the object-naming activity may include people seen on the video. If students have learned adjectives and other modifying forms, they can be asked to describe the objects or people seen on video. If they have learned adverbs of manner or location, they can be asked to describe the location of the objects or people. This may be the case in (2) as well. The objective is to get the students to practice the various verb forms already learned as well as to exercise their judgment on the best alternatives for describing with limited skills and resources. As noted earlier, this is a good chance for the teacher to consider providing students with frames, guided examples or questions, or vocabulary items from which they can pick the ones they may need in describing a specific action or event.

Both (2) and (3) can be done by students on their own or in manageable groups. Such tasks provide students with the opportunity to stretch their imaginations through role-playing or by telling the story from the muted viewing stage. Subsequent viewing need not take valuable class time but can be arranged at a media lab where students can do the viewing at their leisure. Class discussions and projects from videos used as teaching tools can stretch over an extended instructional period. However, the teacher is the best judge of the various steps needed to make a successful transfer of knowledge from the film or video. For example, if the video is shown in the first few weeks of classes, limited time should be reserved for such activities because the level of competency in the language is very low. Discussions should be limited to sentence building and short dialogue. As the students advance in the language, more time can be allocated for longer dialogues or writing projects. As a guide to the effectiveness of the adopted methodology, the teacher may use the students' overall level of enthusiasm in group work and interest in s particular video or film.

3.2 Intermediate Level

At the intermediate level, students can be exposed to the same techniques and methods used for students at the elementary level with additional activities that are more refined and that demand acquired and cumulative abilities. The first viewing (which may be muted), should orient the students to the footage without the benefit of full audio. This would allow the students to build their own storylines. A group discussion should follow the first viewing with the teacher asking both deductive and summative questions. In subsequent viewings, (with audio), the students' attention should be directed to the language use to help them assess how close their initial storyline is to the video or film narrative. Students should then be encouraged to develop an elaborate storyline. At this time, the students should work more independently without pressure from the teacher to produce a storyline which is a replica of the video or film storyline. Minor variations should be encouraged to bring out individualization maximum creativity.

At this level, the teacher may also want to emphasize and test comprehension by encouraging the students to take the initiative to demonstrate their language skills and abilities. The teacher should refrain from offering extensive help to allow them to figure out the story to the best of their abilities. The teacher should refrain from providing pointers that are geared toward influencing students' creative abilities. As students work independently they would have an opportunity to create a storyline which is unique to their experiences. They should not merely transcribe the story as told in the video or film. Alternative approaches can be suggested to reduce the level of dependency on the teacher. Guidance and input from the teacher should weigh more heavily in the areas of vocabulary items, grammar, and sentence structures that reflect the level of proficiency expected. The students can be reminded of specific events or situations in the video or film which can be described using specific sentence patterns, vocabulary items, or grammatical relations that are currently being explored in class. The teacher should, however, make note of sentence structures and grammatical relations that are akin to the ongoing activities and which may have not been introduced in class. These should be introduced as soon as possible. Withholding critical information may be harmful because (once the students develop a structural pattern that is not accurate), changing habitual patterns may prove to be a difficult process.

At the intermediate level, activities may be increased and more group work should be encouraged. In a group, students can help each other to improve their oral proficiency and to develop confidence in using the language without the fear of being corrected by the teacher. Allowing the students to discuss matters without the teacher's input is beneficial as long as the students are up to the challenge and are willing to be creative, supportive, and are willing to work collaboratively. A group discussion—where students can compare notes and ideas—should be followed by a teacher-led class discussion aimed at bringing the cumulative ideas to a desired focus. This can also serve as evaluative and feedback measures.

3.3 Advanced Level

It is at the advanced level that students should be encouraged to be as independent as possible in their creativity with the language, culture, and general knowledge. The expected proficiency would enable the student to sustain a conversation with a native speaker with little difficulty. Consequently, this is the stage at which the teacher should make maximum use of video or film. Critical thinking and creativity is at its best at this stage too; therefore, students can be asked to critique the video show more creativity in their discussion and writing projects. It is always advisable to start the students off with relatively easy tasks and to allow them to develop their language abilities. Priority should be given to videos rich in cultural and general knowledge content. Otherwise, a video should be selected based on its relevance to the contents of the course curriculum and syllabus.

To ensure maximum output, students at this stage should view a video at least twice. During the first viewing, the main objective is to familiarize the students with the contents and context of the video. The second viewing would emphasize attentiveness in order for the students to pick out the salient features from the footage. These salient features should be provided for the students as a viewing guide during their second viewing at the least.

Emphasis should be on comprehension to encourage students to pay attention to audio and video details. In some segments, the narrative pace might appear faster than students are accustomed to. It is important, therefore, to encourage the students to try to pay as much attention as possible to the way the native speakers use the language in natural environments. This is an opportunity that is not readily available in a day-to-day classroom situations even when the teacher is a native speaker of the language. The art of listening is just as important as those of speaking and writing. To facilitate this, students can be provided with pre-designed comprehension questions. Working in groups is advisable because the students would be developing oral and comprehension skills at the same time.

All students should be encouraged to interact with each other as well as with the teacher. The teacher can begin by asking the students deductive questions and then encouraging them to ask informational questions to clear up missed or misunderstood parts of the story. Such an exercise would allow the teacher to provide additional information that may have been overlooked during her or his preparation of the students for the initial viewing stages. Once the teacher is satisfied that all the necessary information has been, he or she can ask the students to work in groups using guidelines which demand both linguistic and factual accuracy. Students are encouraged to work in groups to discuss and ask each other questions about their knowledge or preconceived ideas about the general information and particularly the culture. If the task is performed in a classroom setting, the teacher should make a point of visiting each group as discussion continues. The teacher's group observation is crucial because it provides an excellent basis for feedback on how the students are handling their learning and interactive tasks.

Writing is an important task at this stage too. The instructor is the best judge for the appropriate time to introduce writing. Some may require a writing task after each video or film viewing session. Providing outline of the main features of the footage is a good start in preparing the students for the comprehension and composition tasks. Experience shows that most students prefer writing tasks because they give them a chance to asses their own functional abilities. Success encourages students, helping them to grow proud of themselves when they see that they are increasing their language proficiency. Students also like to show off their creativity with the language. It is a good idea to use writing tasks for book projects or class presentations. This is also a way to encourage the students to discuss their cultural experiences.

4. USE OF CD-ROMS AND OTHER COMPUTER-ASSISTED PROGRAMS

Until recently, there were no CD-ROMs or interactive, multimedia programs available for learning African languages. Most African languages still suffer from a lack of textual learning materials. As a result, the prospect for developing CD-ROMs or multimedia computer programs for these languages seems far-fetched. The major handicap is financial. It is becoming more and more difficult to obtain grants to develop materials for most of the least commonly taught languages including, especially, African languages.

In spite of these problems, however, some African language instructors and a few companies have developed computer-assisted materials and software for the teaching and learning of African languages (unfortunately, only a few of these are commercially available). The purpose of this section is to discuss the need for computer-assisted language learning programs in African languages and then present a brief overview of the very few CD-ROMs and interactive multimedia computer programs available for African language pedagogy. We will concentrate on the programs that can be used on personal computers such as IBM compatibles or Macintosh. There are programs on mainframe computers or servers at various institutions which have not been made accessible to the public.

4.1 The Need for CALL Materials

In general, instructors of less commonly taught languages (LCTLs) face a host of special problems that significantly compromise the effectiveness of their language programs and weaken the national infrastructure of qualified speakers of these languages. Tight budgets and small enrollments limit the number of colleges and universities which can sustain credible instructional programs in such languages, leading to the prevailing situation in which only a select minority of schools in the country can offer comprehensive instruction in African languages. While students enrolled at these schools can readily pursue study of these languages throughout the academic year, many students (both traditional and nontraditional) across the nation have little choice but to go to one of the universities offering the target language and enroll in an intensive summer program. Typically, summer programs cover one level at a time, requiring at least three summers to complete an advanced level.

During the in-between summer period, these students are totally cut off from their summer instructors, language materials for revision, and limited structured opportunities to put the language to use. They can neither sustain their skills enhance their proficiency in the target language. Experience has shown that when the students return to summer study in the following year, they show a marked decline in performance. There is also an alarming attrition rate due to the discouragement the students suffer as they struggle with remaining proficient between summer sessions. It is our opinion that the nation suffers in this regard. There is immeasurable waste of resources in the process of introducing students to critical but less commonly taught languages in a sporadic manner. We are, in essence, failing to meet the needs of these students by luring them to programs that cannot bring them to a level of skill that is sustainable. This "a shot in the arm" mode of language teaching and learning cannot be expected to create a group of lifelong learners of the language.

In many cases, the only native speaker the students encounter is the instructor. Exposure to ways of speech, tone, intonations, gestures, and body language which play a vital role in many of the African languages cannot be adequately taught in a classroom environment through text materials or by coming into contact with only one speaker of the language. This is an unfortunate situation considering that the countries in which the target languages are spoken comprise regions of the world that are largely unfamiliar or to students.

Recognizing that these problems play significant roles in reducing the efficacy of instruction in African languages across the United States, many African language instructors have embarked on the development of computer-assisted language learning materials. Next, we will discuss and describe some of the available CALL materials for African languages.

4.2 Multimedia Interactive CD-ROMs

4.2.1. *Jê K'Á Sæ Yorùbá* Companion CD-ROM

The *Jê K'Á Sæ Yorùbá* Companion CD-ROM was developed at the University of Wisconsin-Madison by Antonia Folarin-Schleicher, a professor of Yoruba and African linguistics. This CD-ROM was the first interactive multimedia language tool for

Antonia Schleicher and Lioba Moshi

an African language in the U.S. It was developed between 1994 and 1996 and published in 1997 (Yale UP) with a companion textbook *Jê K'Á Sœ Yorùbá*, published in 1993 (Yale).

The CD-ROM is designed for use on PC computers with Microsoft Windows 95 or 98. It begins with an introductory video of different scenes in Yorubaland and a song that describe show other West African groups refer to the Yoruba people. Students using this tutorial begin by selecting a specific lesson or module from a menu of lessons. The first page shows the author's picture and a menu that gives students the following options: "Meet Your Teacher," "About the CD-ROM," and "Setup & Orientation." If the user chooses "Meet Your Teacher," a video clip of the author telling learners about herself and the Yoruba people is shown. They may also choose "About the CD-ROM," which tells them about the program.

The entire tutorial utilizes a variety of interactive multimedia teaching strategies. For example, a portion of the preliminary lesson covers the Yoruba alphabet. The alphabet is represented on the screen in the form of clickable objects. The learner can click on any of the letters of the alphabet to hear how it sounds. As the student clicks on a letter, a recording icon shows up in the form of a tape recorder. The student can click the Record button to record his or her pronunciation of the letter just spoken, click the Stop button to stop the recording, click the Play button to play back his or her voice, and click the Check button to hear a native speaker's voice pronouncing the same sound. Students can use this recording system for any of the activities in the program. Being able to do this on their own gives them control of their own learning. They do not have to wait for a teacher in class to teach them the alphabet or other aspects of grammar treated on the CD-ROM. They can always video or audio clips if they need to practice without having to rewind a tape over and over. Every aspect of the program is available to them by clicking a convenient button.

After the alphabet and titles of address are dealt with, video clips of different people greeting one another at different times of the day can be accessed. Cultural notes explaining the different gestures that accompany the greetings are presented. The role of greetings is also explained. Each lesson has a cultural theme with lots of cultural information. Similarly, every lesson ends with culture tidbits. This cultural information is of value to scholars in anthropology, history, political science, religious studies, folklore, cultural studies, and for other Africanists who are interested in the Yoruba people. When a topic deals, for example, with the traditional ruling system in Yorubaland, video clips of a traditional king and his chiefs are presented to show learners the modern setting of a Yoruba king's palace. There are also video clips on the open market system in Yorubaland. Students can watch how Yoruba people haggle in the market on a day-to-day basis. The CD-ROM provides the opportunity for students not only to learn how to speak the language, but also to learn facts about the Yoruba people in general. Some of the knowledge acquired through this CD-ROM can be useful in their different disciplines such history, anthropology, literature, folklore, cultural studies, etc.

The interactive nature of this multimedia program makes it possible for students to acquire a lot of information on their own outside the class. Students can spend as much time as they like interacting with their teacher in this "virtual classroom." Real class time can now be spent on difficult aspects of the language or other factual information that the students have problems with.

4.2.2 *Jé K'A Ka Yoruba* Multimedia Yoruba CD-ROM

Since the release of the inaugural CD-ROM and accompanying textbook, the same author has developed another CD-ROM and textbook for intermediate-level Yoruba, and is currently developing similar materials for the advanced level. Intermediate and advanced materials expand on the first-year materials. For example, the intermediate and Advanced CD-ROMs are developed with the following improvements:

- **Speech recognition functionality**: The CD-ROMs analyze students' recorded speech and provide them with feedback on their accuracy in pronunciation. The speech recognition feature can also be used for dialogues. Students can assume one role or author in the dialogues.

- **Cross-platform compatibility**: The CD-ROMs from this package will run equally well on Macintosh and PC-compatible computers, making the curriculum accessible to a larger audience. The elementary-level CD-ROM runs only on PCs.

- **User control**: More navigation buttons, along with feedback about where a student is in the CD-ROM's structure, will maximize the interactive potential of this medium. The CD-ROM allows the creation of a preference file for each student, storing useful information for future sessions. And the QuickTime video format can be used to allow students to instantly rewind, fast forward, or jump to any point in a sound or video clip.

- **World Wide Web component**: The developers intend to create and maintain a Web site where instructors or students can find content updates and corrections, links to up-to-date cultural information available online, and tips for maximizing the potential of the CD-ROM. For example, there will be links from the CD-ROMs to a *Jê K'Á Sæ Yorùbá* Companion Web Page that has links to various sites which relate to the cultural notes or other topics in the CD-ROM lessons. Large multimedia clips can be accessed from the CD-ROM, while the Web can be used only for easily downloadable information and existing Web resources. Therefore, this project will take advantage of the respective strengths of CD-ROMs and the World Wide Web, without making any compromises based on the limitations of either medium.

- **Enhanced electronic communication:** A new Yoruba font, already developed and to be included with future releases, will allow students to interact with the CD-ROM more easily using the keyboard, practice their writing and speaking skills, and facilitate email and World Wide Web communication Yoruba students and scholars locally and across the nation.

- **Expandable architecture:** The CD-ROMs will be designed so that additional lesson content can be added easily. Instructors and students will be able to write their own questions and answers, tailoring their learning to their environments and increasing their engagement with the curriculum.

- **Application to other languages:** Not just an observable model, but a usable template for future projects, the CD-ROM with its expandable architecture will allow conversion to other languages with unprecedented ease. Instructors will need only basic computer skills to "plug in" text, audio, and video content, with programming expertise needed only for a relatively small portion of the development cycle.

After the CD-ROMs are pressed, the whole program will still be kept in an external drive to allow for revisions or migration of data to a future medium other than from CD-ROM if desirable.

4.2.3 The Significance of the Yoruba CD-ROMs

One major significance of this project is that through these model CD-ROMs, a LCTL which otherwise might not be available to students for lack of funding will be made available across the nation. Schools that otherwise will not offer the course may elect to share instructors by making the CD-ROMs available to their students and having them attend the online office hours with their instructors on the Internet. It is important to note that the interactive aspect of language learning, with an expert in the field is still essential, hence the online office hours with learners who do not have access to an instructor on-site.

Equally important, the project will directly benefit students by providing enhanced learning. The first-year Yoruba CD-ROM exposes students to dozens of native speakers in genuine West African contexts while at the same time providing them with the language suitable for their level. Hundreds of sound clips and videos demonstrate subtleties of verbal expression while the recording feature of the CD-ROM teaches students to evaluate their own speech progress. All of these benefits come from a lively, culturally-rich interactive program that learners enjoy to use. As a result, students (of LCTLs) will not have the problem of encountering only their instructors since the CD-ROMs will expose them to different native speakers of the language.

In addition, students have a better chance of being in control of their own learning, since the materials can be used in both traditional and nontraditional learning settings. The reality of self-managed learning becomes more feasible when students do not have to wait until the next class meeting before using the language in a meaningful way.

In the few schools where instructors are available, the CD-ROMs can be used to enhance classroom instruction by allowing the CD-ROMs to take care of many activities that waste classroom time. In addition, they can also be used to enhance listening, oral, and reading skills. With funds from the University of Wisconsin-Madison, Schleicher was also able to develop special Yoruba fonts that will now permit learners from across the nation to write Yoruba characters using email or the Web. With this font, CD-ROM activities can be linked to an online discussion space for any class. Topics for discussion could be posted by the instructor while learners post written materials (comments or compositions) for discussion or peer review. As a result, the CD-ROM and the WWW can be used to enhance the acquisition of various communicative skills. This medium allows students to learn at their own pace and in their own different ways. Slower students can spend more time with the computer (the patient helper), and faster students can race ahead.

The impact of these materials also goes beyond learners' college years. The materials can continue to serve as resources for students who aim at becoming lifelong learners.

4.2.4 *Beginner Zulu* CD-ROM

Beginner Zulu CD-ROM was developed and published (1997) by Interactive Tutor Company in South Africa. It is aimed at teaching how to speak Zulu. It has three main sections: cultural diversity, phonics, and phrasing and vocabulary.

In the cultural diversity section, there is narration on why Zulu speakers do things the way they do. Cultural differences between Zulu speakers and white South Africans are explored to provide a better understanding of them. The next section deals with phonics, providing an explanation of how to produce certain Zulu sounds such as clicks in order to pronounce Zulu words correctly. The last section explores phrases and vocabulary items that are relevant to the environment and different situations.

The CD-ROM is designed for use on PC computers with Microsoft Windows or Windows NT 3.5, Windows 95, or higher. It has audio, images, but no videos. The only native speaker whom learners are exposed to is the narrator who talks about the cultural diversity, phonics, phrases, and vocabulary.

4.2.5 *Learn Zulu* and *Learn Xhosa* CD-ROMs

Both *Learn Zulu* and *Learn Xhosa* are CD-ROMs developed by Eurotalk Interactive Company, based in London. These CD-ROMs belong to a series of developed for "absolute beginners." They contain essential words and phrases and are designed for people who want to learn these languages quickly. According to Eurotalk interactive, these CD-ROMs are "addictive, fun, and make learning easy." They are meant for those who do not have the time to become fluent in the language, but need the basics in a hurry.

The CD-ROMs include topics such as first words, phrases, food, shopping, numbers, and time. They are interactive in the sense that there are immediate responses to whatever choices a learner makes. Learners can compare their pronunciation with

162

native speakers' pronunciation if they use the recording option. There are easy and hard quizzes plus a challenging memory game. Students can keep track of their total scores on activities, and they can print their own awards. The CD-ROMs also contain on-screen help and an online dictionary that they can print out for handy reference. They have audio, images, but no videos.

The minimum system requirements for PC are VGA with 256 colors, sound card, 486 processor or above, 8Mb RAM, CD-ROM drive, and a microphone; for Macintosh the requirements are multimedia capabilities, System 7 or higher and Microsoft Word 6.0 or higher. CD-ROMs are Windows and Mac compatible (see Eurotalk 1998).

4.3 Computer-Assisted Language Instructional Materials for Hausa and Wolof

Multimedia exercises and activities for Hausa and Wolof were developed by Russ Schuh, a professor of Hausa and African linguistics at the UCLA. The materials are intended for beginning and intermediate students. They were designed as supplements to regular classroom instruction, but they have potential as a basis for self-instruction for those who do not have access to regular classes.

The materials require a Macintosh computer running system 7.0 or higher and Hypercard version 2.1 or higher. They will run satisfactorily on a Macintosh SE or Classic, but faster computers provide better results. They have been tested on a Power Macintosh and run well in this environment too. The computer should have an internal or external hard disk with at least five

163

MB of space and preferably 20 MB. The full set of exercises for each language requires about 20 MB, but a subset of the exercises can be used if disk space is limited.

The exercises provide a multimedia environment in the form of digitized sound, text, graphics, and limited animation. They are interactive, giving feedback to correct and incorrect responses. They level practice in pronunciation, vocabulary, grammar, and listening comprehension. To easy, error-free navigation, all exercises are accessed through an index which allows students to select topics for study. Students may return to the index at any time if they wish to move on to other exercises. All exercises have a similar format, with a menu which allows students to explore the exercise, take a tutorial on the points covered in the exercise, or go directly to the exercise. The exercises themselves use a variety of techniques, including typed responses by students, clicking at certain locations, and dragging objects.

The development of these multimedia materials began around 1990 with support from U.S. Department of Education Title VI grants and a grant from the UCLA Office of Instructional Development. Exercise conception was by Russell Schuh, with most design and Hypercard programming techniques by Anne Wysocki. Language consultants were Lawan Yalwa and Abdullahi Bature for Hausa and Dieynaba Gaye for Wolof. The exercises are free as shareware and are available for instructional use only (see Schuh 1995).

4.4 Media-Driven Language Learning System (MDLS)

The MDLS for teaching Kiswahili was created by John Mugane (1999), a professor of Swahili and African linguistics, while at Stanford University. It was created by using Multimedia Director and it is intended as a general purpose application for storytelling, documentary, reporting, and movie watching for language learning and literacy. MDLS uses pictures, graphics, and QuickTime videos which facilitate the text, induce conversation, and allow participation of learners who may opt to hear individual word pronunciation simply by clicking on them. The application is versatile in its function and audio track and the text may be replaced in order to include other languages while playing the same movies.

The system provides QuickTime movies and graphics, in slide-show format with text appearing on screen as the presentation advances. MDLS is used for comprehension purposes where students watch film, read text, listen to sounds and practice the pronunciations of words, phrases, paragraphs. Learners also type their responses to comprehension issues and questions.

The short QuickTime movies and slides are referred to as modules within MDLS. In one lesson, there can be as many as five modules dealing with matters such as transportation, stories, Matatu/Daladala, Nairobi, and the environment. The transportation module call up a movie that shows a moving vehicle with a caption below. Captioning enables the learner to be able to relate what they are hearing to what they are seeing and how it is written. Captioning can be turned on and off. Exploiting visual and audio cues in this manner capitalizes on forming associations between the text, the sound, and the pictures or video.

165

Upon watching an entire clip, the students may opt to view the associated text without watching the movie again. It is in this environment that learners will be able to click on individual words and hear their pronunciations. Swahili-English glossaries are also available as well as cultural and grammar notes. An accompanying textbook *Tujifunze Kiswahili* (*Let's Learn Kiswahili*) by Aramati Digital Technologies Publications (1999) is also available.

It is important to stress that no CD-ROM or any computer mediated learning material can entirely take the place of the classroom instructor, nor would we want one to if it could. These computer materials were designed, instead, to enhance the quality of the classroom time, to make efficient, effective, and meaningful use of this precious resource. The students' independent work with the computer materials will equip them with a consistent level of background information and core skills, allowing the instructor to teach at a much higher level. And students themselves, especially the naturally reticent ones, can be expected to participate more in class since the materials will give them valuable practice in listening and speaking.

For learners who want to use the computer materials for independent courses, an "online office hour" can be set up in conjunction with the CALL materials.

5. USING BULLETIN BOARDS, CHAT ROOMS, AND WEB SITES

There are a number of other pioneering instructional technology projects around the country intended to enhance the teaching of

African languages. When completed, the results of these projects will provide ways for teachers to maximize the learning opportunities of their students using interactive media. The results will also create a platform from which participating institutions can transform their African language teaching and learning environments.

While the field of African languages will rely more and more on disseminating materials on CD-ROM, it is challenged in its agenda for the twenty-first century to produce real authentic and affordable CDs for the various languages. In addition, it will have to think through on the best and most efficient way of utilizing multimedia teaching tools options. These may include the direct use of the Internet and (1) bulletin boards where teachers can leave instructions for projects and check results; and (2) computer chat-rooms- where students can develop all three of the major skills: speaking, listening, and writing; (3) Web sites where interactive video or film can be utilized.

Bulletin boards, chat rooms, and web sites are relatively easy to set up and o manage and can be very effective for teaching and learning (Moshi and Ojo 2000). Teachers and students alike can use these media as avenues for discussing cultural or general topics. The advantage of computer-based instruction is that it encourages student-centered teaching and student-managed learning and can serve as non-traditional classrooms which can put to practice both the teacher-centered and student-centered modes of instruction.

Bulletin boards   The appeal of bulletin boards as a venue for language instruction comes from the possibility of having a low-key moderated discussion between students while the teacher is minimally involved. As such, a discussion on a film or video shown in class or viewed independently in a media lab can be conducted on the bulletin-board. The teacher can choose to be a moderator or can appoint a discussion leader for a specified period of time. The duration of a topic can be pre-determined or not; in other words, the teacher or discussion leader can determine when the discussion of a specific topic should be terminated. Bulletin board discussions can also be carried out over several days and can be stored either as new, unread, or saved messages in a folder that can be accessed by the teacher. It can also be printed for use in future classroom discussions. The advantages also include the possibility of using the discussions as an evaluation and/or feedback on individual as well as group progress.

Chat rooms The computer chat room, which is real-time, serves as a conversation forum where all participating members remain engaged in the discussion for as long as they are logged in. The nature of a discussion can be pre-determined, but at best it should be left free like a normal conversation. Here students are less guarded and can see and correct each other's mistakes. In order for this medium to work well where enrollments are larger than ten, it is necessary to designate chat room hours for a group of students. Designating specific chat room hours is to ensure that a conversation does take place. Unlike the bulletin board where materials can be posted, the discussion in chat rooms requires instantaneous responses. The teacher can take part in a chat room discussion by staying online at the same time to provide feedback on the content, grammar, or vocabulary. When used well, it can be a lot of fun while at the same time students are learning from each other (Moshi and Ojo 2000).

The Internet can also be a forum for the training of non-professional teachers (in many cases teaching assistants and part-time instructors). It can be used by professional and non-professional teachers to: (A) enrich their pedagogical bases; (B) increase their abilities to use interactive media technologies; (C) demonstrate how one can incorporate culture and general knowledge into language instruction; and (D) conduct language and culture proficiency tests. The expected outcome is tantamount to killing many birds with one stone. It would also be a repository for authentic teaching and learning materials which would, undoubtedly, enhance the way African languages are taught on any campus in the U.S.

MOOs Another consideration which can impact the field of African language instruction is the development of a Multi-user Object Oriented software (MOO). A MOO is established to provide both synchronous and hypertext forms of communication through the internet.[8] A MOO offers the same experience as the computer chat room except that it is more organized and can involve participants—of teachers and learners—from multiple institutions. The format would allow students and teachers to meet for real-time sessions using text-based interaction. All interactions that occur on the internet can be recorded using an online recorder. A built-in mechanism also allows the instructor to forward to students already scripted interactions using personal email accounts or an account specifically opened for students in class (or in a learning group).[9] There is also a built-in mechanism which

8. At the University of Georgia and the University of Pennsylvania, a similar mechanism is available through the University computing system in a program nicknamed Web-CT (Web-site Computer Education Technology) for the purpose of on-line instruction. Faculty create a course-page which may contain a section for course materials, on-line chat, a bulletin-board, test and exercise sites, a forum site and a personal e-mail site. These can be accessed by students using their own user-id name and a password established by the teacher for the whole class. Teachers post notes and assignments, students use the bulletin-board for a specific class discussion, and the chat-room to debate on issues which are deemed current and relevant to a designated topic.

9. The language Learning Framework (acronym: LLF) was conceptualized by a group of LCTL (Less Commonly Taught Languages)

169

allows the teacher to preview students' activities on the account, set tests, and grade student work. Feedback can be accomplished via a combination of the Internet or direct contact in a classroom setting where print-outs of students' activities can be distributed for discussion and review.

The design also allows materials at the MOO object site to be changed, increased, decreased, or tailored, to meet the needs of the participating students. A provision can also be made to divide the students into groups based on their proficiency levels while appropriate materials and tests are selected to match their abilities. Thus is extremely useful when a class of students appears to exhibit diversity in skills and learning strategies among the students. Students who have a hard time grasping specific materials can be assisted without slowing down those who are meeting the expected proficiency requirements at a particular level.

Pedagogical activities may include, but are not limited to, the following:

1. **Outright instruction** in which a student or a group of students receive interactive language instruction. While online,

---

task force members who were charged with the responsibility of proposing a learner-managed foreign language learning framework for the 90% of the languages of the world currently taught in schools in the United States. The project, funded by Ford Foundation, was further developed by different language fields which constitute the membership of the National Council on Less Commonly Taught Languages (NCOLCTL), Each group was expected to develop a Language Learning Framework that addressed the needs of that language, while preserving the common theme binding all LCTLs. The basic notion of LLF is that language instruction should be content-based and student oriented. The teacher serves only as a facilitator and the content should be authentic. The learner should be guided to use the content to develop his or her communicative skill depending less on forms (mainly grammar) and the functions (how the forms are used).

the teacher can teach any subject matter, guiding the student through the needed interactions. For example, at the elementary level, the teacher can teach greetings, guiding the student through the appropriate responses. This can be done by issuing specific instructions at the beginning of the encounter and by reinforcing their strengths as the interaction progresses. This can be modeled on the same techniques used in the classroom when the teacher instructs students on how to respond to a specific form of greeting. The only difference is that all is done through an online chat instead of face-to-face in a classroom setting.

2. **Impromptu interactions** in which students interact and exchange ideas through an online conversation model. This is allows a face-to-face encounter even though the MOO interactions are text-based instead of oral. Many speech-like features such as open and closed conversations, holding the floor, turn-taking, taking the floor (including how to avoid or handle interruptions), making requests, and performing other speech acts, would be used. There should be a designated discussion leader to initiate the conversation each week. This does not mean that no new ideas could be brought into the discussion; rather, the discussion leader should ensure that topic continuity is maintained and that subtopics are fully integrated into the designated topic.

3. **Role play** in which special topics can be assigned to students using the MOO software. Each student could be given an opportunity to select a topic and adopt a role for which he or she would conduct a conversation. Such topics may be specific or not and might include topics such as buying and

selling; market or shop scenes; doctor-patient conversations; activities at a postal service and other financial management centers (buying/selling, mailing, depositing money, withdrawing money, buying money orders, sending a telegram, fax, etc.); teacher-student interactions; and student-student interactions (conversations on a variety of academic, social, political, and other related matters of interest to students);

4. **Writing tasks** which may involve collaborative writing. Students would be allowed to construct a piece of text in pairs or more (not to exceed four participants in one group). Guided topics or student-selected topics would be encouraged. This format might also be used for collaborative projects between students of the same institution or across institutions. Reading-comprehension exercises in which students would provide written responses can be featured here. This includes activities related to video descriptions, online journals, topic analysis, letter writing, to name only a few.

5. **Instruction and teacher assistance:** A MOO is also designed to have a teacher-on-call at the main site (initially at the University of Georgia and the University of Pennsylvania). An individual will monitor student activities on the site, and from time to time will interact with the students online at specified times. The specific times for such interactions would be posted at the welcome page to enable the students to reach the teacher for special online instruction. A teacher-on-call would not only monitor the individual student's activity at the site, the participating institutions, the rate and frequency of activity, the originating station, and the number of specific participants who make contact with an instructor on call, but will also offer assistance to non-professional

teachers online. Such contacts could be used to discuss the materials posted on the site, ways in which a specific concept could be handled for maximum impact on the learner, teaching approach, and handling student's learning needs. The advantage of using this medium lies in the fact that it is directly linked to the operating context (the students learning, the materials being used and the environment in which the learning and teaching activities are situated). The teacher on call and the student or instructor can access the sites at the same time for reference as they communicate online. This is by far more efficient than the use of a conventional telephone, email system, or other media. For review purposes, the teacher on call would also document the pattern in which he or she interacts with individual participants, the nature of contacts, the assistance provided, the subject matters covered, and the recurring patterns of assistance solicited from students. Such documentation could be used for teacher training using MOO, initiating needed changes on the design of the materials used in MOOs, and designing additional or supplemental materials.

The Web could be used to generate multimedia, context-based exercises for: (1) the teacher to reinforce different language skills; (2) the students to self-assess their progress; and (3) the teacher to monitor the student's proficiency at a given stage. The teacher-student link can be established through the MOO interface, or other Internet connections. Students can use email or telnet responses to their instructors who could, in turn, e-mail or telnet the feedback.

The Web can consist of several parts whose foci are well distributed in the main areas of required proficiency: a focus on listening-comprehension (through built-in audio capability), reading-comprehension exercises, and writing. Students could also monitor their own progress on listening comprehension and to some extent reading comprehension. In a listening-comprehension segments, the student could be asked a set of comprehension questions for which he or she could respond orally or in writing. He or she would be prompted for each response. The instructor could also use the Internet to monitor the reading and writing segments as well as provide feedback.

As multimedia resources, CD-ROMs, the Web and MOOs could be used together to provide students with rich content and authentic materials. Lessons might feature specific themes which the students could explore by listening to a narration and linking to related videos. At the end of a lesson, students could be provided with several options which might include connecting to the MOO software and then the Web site. Students can be given an opportunity to discuss the subject matter (cultural implications, general knowledge), role-play, perform a writing task, or do some writing exercises on the Web. Selected still-frames from the CD-ROM could also be posted on the WEB to help students recall specific linguistic and cultural matters on the CD-ROM.

The use of the Internet will surpass workshops and institutional teacher training endeavors that are aimed at transforming teaching strategies for African languages. It will be an avenue through which students learn from each other and from teachers outside of their institutions. Teachers will also use the Internet for collaborative projects, developing teaching materials as well as learning materials. The business of teaching and language learning will gain a more unified and sophisticated format that advocates a language learning framework suitable for modern foreign language teaching and learning.

CHAPTER EIGHT

A Twenty-First Century Vision for African Language Instruction and Learning

1. BACKGROUND

In this chapter, we will focus on ALTA, its field development activities, and the ways in which it is attempting to address the needs of the field, particularly its role as the voice of authority for the field.

The field of African languages has benefited greatly from the development of ALTA, founded in 1988. At that time, its membership consisted primarily of faculty with affiliations to Title VI African Studies Centers and who often served as African language coordinators. ALTA's primary function was to co-ordinate summer language programs and explore ways in which the resources that were provided by U.S. Department of Education Title VI grants could be shared to benefit the development and advancement of African languages taught at only those institutions with Title VI funding.

It was not until 1990 (when the association had its first non-Title VI president[10]) that the shift was made to make it include all African language teaching across the nation as well as internationally. Currently, ALTA membership includes many teachers from non-Title VI institutions in the United States and some in Africa, Europe, Asia, and Latin America.

ALTA's success in building a diverse membership follows from the goals that were set forth from the onset. ALTA's main goal was to professionalize the teaching of African languages, both nationally and internationally. This was done by broadening ALTA's membership, holding annual workshops and semiannual meetings, and the publication of a newsletter popularly known as *LUGHA*. The annual and semiannual meetings or workshops were held in conjunction with major national and international conferences, including the Annual Conference on African Studies (ASA), the Annual Conference on African Linguistics (ACAL), and one time in conjunction with the International Conference on Pragmatics (an annual event at the University of Illinois, Urbana-Champaign). The workshop focused on teaching method-

10. The ALTA President (1990-94) was Dr. Lioba Moshi (University of Georgia—with non-Title VI African Studies Center), who succeeded Dr. John Hutchinson (Boston University– with a Title VI African Studies Center). Dr. Moshi is currently the Director of the African Studies Center which offers a Certificate in African Studies, and has a core of twenty faculty distributed across disciplines (humanities & sciences). She also oversees the teaching of three African languages, Swahili, Yoruba, and Zulu.

ologies, teaching resources, uses of technologies, and the development of software that addresses the teaching needs of specific African languages (starting with the more commonly taught African languages: Hausa, Swahili, Yoruba).

ALTA has also enjoyed this success due to its energetic administrative board which has produced impressive accomplishments: a growing membership, the establishment of language-specific task forces, a newsletter, annual professional development workshops, annual conferences, and a sustainable budget generated from membership fees.

An important period of this development began with the National Council of Organizations of Less Commonly Taught Languages (NCOLCTL) whose major grant from the Ford Foundation facilitated the turnaround in the field of LCTLs. ALTA, like many other LCTLs, received support from NCOLCTL through a major grant from the Ford Foundation. The funds were earmarked for the support of ALTA's rapid field development. The cornerstone was the development of the language learning framework (footnote 4) whose goal was to seek collective solutions to problems in foreign language pedagogy as applied to the LCTLs.

With advice and support from NCOLCTL, ALTA embarked on three language-field development projects involving Hausa, Swahili, and Yoruba. These languages formed task forces whose shared goal was to professionalize the field. Major undertakings included the development of a better understanding of specific language needs, the needs of the learners in particular. The implementation objective was to agree on curricula and activities that meet that need. The framework was intended to guide the production of real results such as teacher training, pedagogical research, textbook design, teaching with technology, and data collection on the numerous African language programs in the

United States (see chapter two). The data served as a reference for numerous discussions by teachers on field needs and goals that will enable the field to evolve into an even more respectable profession. All these developments, the development of the African Language Learning Framework in particular, would not have been possible had it not been for the three years of funding from the Ford Foundation through NCOLCTL.

The outcomes include an interactive Hausa video, a cultural curriculum, enhanced intensive language and culture study abroad programs, and the development of a rationale for the study of Hausa at institutions of higher learning. The Swahili task force embarked on the preparation of a teacher's manual (Moshi, et al. 1999) which addresses issues of methodology and a student's manual intended to instruct students on the best ways to exploit student-centered learning, the development of multimedia software[11], interactive video[12], and data collection on over 100 Swahili language programs in the U.S. Data collection was also undertaken by the Yoruba task force in addition to the development of a generic goal-driven syllabus, a Yoruba cultural course, and an interactive CD-ROM[13] which has gained both a national and international prestige and popularity (see 4.2).

11. This is an on-going project which was initiated by Dr. John Mugane while at Stanford University (now a professor at Ohio University). Its end goal is to provide an integrated software that can be used by both elementary and intermediate Swahili learners.

12. cf. Moshi, Lioba (1996) *Kiswahili: Lugha na Utamaduni--* a set of eight videos covering twenty three lessons with authentic Swahili language and a variety of themes of contemporary life in East Africa, particularly Tanzania. These videos are available from the University of Georgia Office of Instructional Support and Development. An accompanying textbook is published by Dunwood Press (1999), Hyattsville, Maryland, and work on an accompanying workbook is already progress.

13. The video *Jé K' A So Yorubá* and its accompanying textbook serve as standard resources for the teaching of Yoruba.

Both ALTA and NCOLCTL expect that this development will continue as the task forces forge new ways of developing sustainable self-sufficiency. Of highest priority is the development of intensive language and culture study abroad programs for all the languages taught in the United States. It is imperative that such a program would move beyond the Yoruba, Swahili and Hausa. Two new task forces, one for a group of West African languages (Bambara, Akan, Fulfulde, and Wolof) and another intended to serve several Southern African languages (Zulu, Xhosa, Shona, Bemba, and Tswana) has also been established.

Most success has been realized in the creation of workshops for which speakers are invited to discuss issues related to teaching and learning. They include an overview of the use of discourse in language teaching and learning, the role of culture, the language learning framework, the field of African language programming in the United States, and computer-assisted language teaching and learning. In 1997, ALTA inaugurated its international conference on language teaching at the University of Wisconsin. Its success was realized by the choice of the conference theme "Defining the Field of African Language Learning and Teaching." The conference attracted a number of American and foreign participants who presented papers on pedagogy as well as teaching with technology. The second annual conference (1998), which focused on the needs and resources of African language learners, teachers, and programs in the United States, and which was hosted by Michigan State University, was equally successful.[14] The third conference (1999) whose theme was "Facing the Winds of Change: The Teaching and Learning of African Languages in the New

14. Proceedings from these two conferences as well as subsequent conferences will be published by Global Publications, Binghamton University, Binghamton.

Millennium" was considered historic because it marked the end of the millennium. It was also a bittersweet achievement for the Association because it managed, for the first time, to persuade a historically black university (HBU), Howard University, to host the conference. This is the only HBU that teaches African languages and which, at one time, held a Title VI-funded African Studies Center. Interestingly, little was known before this conference about the institutional commitment to the teaching of African languages and culture even though the instruction of African languages holds a low priority compared to the CTLs at this institution. Nevertheless, ALTA considers these small steps to be tremendous achievements and expects continuous success in the twenty first century to attract worldwide attention. To do so, ALTA must have coherent strategic plans.

2. NATIONAL STRATEGIC PLANNING IN AFRICAN LANGUAGES

The U.S. national focus on Africa is at its highest right now. Following President Clinton's visits to Africa in 1998 and 2000, policy makers, educators, and the business community have embarked on an intensive search for ways to re-link with the continent. The President's visit was followed by Regional Africa Summits held in 1998 and 1999, and the National Summit (chaired by President Clinton) was held in Washington DC, February 16-18, 2000. All the summits focused on a new look at education and culture, democracy and human rights, economic and sustainable development, humanitarian assistance, ecology, and conflict resolution. The theme, which will resonate across the Pacific to the continent of Africa, regards the development of an understanding, cooperation, and sustainable partnerships with the continent of Africa. The expected outcome is a firmer link with the African peoples on the continent and the Diaspora, the development of economic ties, and a promotion of sustainable educational and technological links with Africa.

These new directions demand a national capability to train and maintain, at a minimum, a segment of the population with the cultural and linguistic knowledge needed to communicate with Africa. This means that African language teachers have to take part in the national dialogue to ensure that those who are involved in these initiatives are well prepared for these tasks and challenges. We have to learn from others who have made mistakes that have derailed national efforts to create national capacities to teach and learn African languages. The field of foreign language instruction offers us a clear example of national efforts which, though laudable, have met with limited success. Competence in foreign language is restricted to only a selected few American's today, generally involving the big three commonly taught languages (French, German, Spanish). The idea of introducing another language into this mix is often resisted, and the call for English as "the international language" is often echoed by policy makers.

ALTA is faced with the enormous task of convincing policy makers of the rationale for teaching African languages to American students and future policy makers instead of embarking on a mission to "anglocize" the continent by instituting English as a Second Language programs on the continent. Policy makers are not blind to the fact that approximately 94% of college language enrollments and 98% of secondary school language enrollments are in the big three languages. ALTA also needs to realize that the recent spate of initiatives such as the National Security Education Program have placed emphasis on the introduction of Arabic, Chinese, Japanese, Russian, and Korean into the schools. Furthermore the creation of three regional-focus National Foreign Language Resource Centers within Title VI of the Higher Education Act is intended to provide some focus on language study, but the special opportunities in foreign language initiatives of the National Endowment for the Humanities are focused on Arabic, Chinese, Japanese, and Russian. The question is, where is the continent of Africa? How can we put the giant foot of Africa in the door? ALTA has to respond to these questions in a formidable national strategic plan for the teaching of African languages.

2.1 National Needs

The national needs for African languages include adequate numbers of experts with specific skills and credible levels of competence in a given language. Without a national curriculum, it is impossible to talk about credible competence which we would define as the ability to perform a range of occupationally, professionally, and socially relevant tasks with peoples of the target language both in Africa and outside of Africa. It should be ALTA's goal to prepare its African language learners to perform adequately in tasks which may include interpersonal or interpretative communication diplomatic, business, academic, scientific, and domestic social services environments. Diverse curricula and teaching methodologies within one language do not lead to the production of credible levels of competence except when the learner is able to obtain all of his or her language training from one institution. Considering that undergraduate education can be obtained from one school and subsequent training at another school, it is imperative that ALTA address the issue of curricular uniformity, comprehensive pedagogical expertise, and the development of special skills that would enhance its field development programs. Traditional forms of language instruction should be considered outdated as we turn to the use of technology to enhance the teaching and learning of African languages. ALTA should encourage its members to adopt the teaching and learning methods discussed in chapters three and four.

In the assessment of national needs, ALTA has to view needs differently from how it did in the past when the goal was a general one as found in all foreign languages: to provide general education. "To fulfill a language requirement" has been the rationale behind the teaching of foreign languages in high schools and college campuses. African language teachers cannot afford to teach an African language solely to satisfy a language requirement. Two or three semesters of language instruction does not do the language or the general knowledge rationale any justice. Thus, the rationale for future teaching of African languages should go beyond personal fulfillment, the promotion of cultural awareness, and developing an understanding of linguistic systems. Considering that only a small minority of students go beyond the required two years (some three semesters, often discontinuous) of college language study, ALTA has an obligation to clearly chart a professional demand (on the part of its experts and skill needs) for credible competence that recognizes the efforts put into the teaching and learning of African languages.

There is also a growing Diaspora community whose language demands are going to go beyond those traditionally found on college campuses. This means that ALTA has to link its college programs with the community to strengthen the teaching of African languages in elementary, middle, and high schools. Presently this sector is very weak concerning expertise and teaching materials. Domestically, there is an increase in the number of first-generation immigrants from Africa who are culturally conscious and who prefer their children to grow up bilingual (English and mother tongue). Many of these children will soon go to college and may (based on current trends for the few who are now in college) will select their mother tongue to fulfill their foreign language requirements, a popular trend in Chinese, Korean, Hindi, and Vietnamese. ALTA can learn from these groups, experiences.

2.2 National Capacities

As noted earlier, the continent of Africa is rapidly emerging as new economic giant. The world will soon be compelled to examine its capacity to respond to the demands for competencies in particular African languages, regardless of the fact that ESL will be marketed heavily to Africa. Demands for competence in particular languages will include the ability to create or strengthen instruction in key languages other than Hausa, Swahili, or Yoruba. National capacity for African languages should be seen as the ability to respond to the constant, changing needs of the world, particularly America and Europe. The African languages national capacities should take advantage of America's superpower status to exploit an American language policy that should be global in nature. Policy makers often argue for national interests which cannot overlook the creation and maintenance of language specialists capable of dealing with the changing world. ALTA should take its cues from this by creating and maintaining language specialists who are capable of dealing with the growing demands in the field of African languages with a broad range of cultures on the continent and the Diaspora.

We are, therefore, advocating an aggressive approach in which ALTA may ensure that the language teachers for each sub-field is an expert. To facilitate this, each sub-field (Swahili, Yoruba, Bambara, Shona, etc.) must have a clear knowledge of itself, who is who, what is needed, how to achieve goals, and where development is most necessary. This entails charging the various task forces to place additional resources in data collection (personal, materials, student enrollments, student needs and wants), and to assess the steps required to strengthen the sub-field. This should feed into the field-wide assessment and development plans which comprise the greater role of ALTA in centralizing expertise, maintaining its strategic planning process, centralizing coordinating mechanisms, and, most of all, strengthening the field-wide Language Learning Framework.

3. PROFESSIONALIZATION

Dwyer (1995) notes that one of the major accomplishments of ALTA between 1990 and 1995 was the development of three National Language Task Forces on Hausa (chaired by Linda Hunter, University of Wisconsin-Madison), Swahili (chaired by Lioba Moshi, University of Georgia-Athens), and Yoruba (chaired by Antonia Schleicher, University of Wisconsin-Madison). He states that "the primary goal of these task forces is to establish the TEACHING of their respective African language as a legitimate and professional discipline."

In 1996 at the ALTA plenary speech, during the annual ALTA meeting in Gainesville, Eyamba Bokamba also emphasized the need to establish the teaching of African languages as a legitimate and professional discipline. Without any doubt and based on these observations, the direction that ALTA should adopt for the twenty-first century must emphasize the importance of establishing the teaching of African languages as a professional discipline. This can be done by eliminating the view that the language teaching is merely a service arm of linguistic or literature departments, or of other area studies programs. This need will become clear as we discuss the concept of professionalism in the context of African languages and as a field development role for ALTA.

3.1 What Is Professionalism?

Darling-Hammond and Goodwin state that

> . . . becoming a profession is neither a dichotomous event nor a state of grace clearly granted to an occupation. Rather, it describes points along a continuum representing the extent to which members of an occupation share a common body of knowledge and use shared standards of practice in exercising that knowledge and use shared standards of practice in exercising that knowledge on behalf of clients. (1993, 20)

A profession incorporates specialized knowledge, self-regulation, special attention to the unique need of clients, autonomous performance, and responsibility for client welfare (Darling-Hammond 1990a). Here are some common beliefs and behaviors associated with the notion of professionalism (Becker 1962; Darling-Hammond 1990a; Goodlad 1990a; Darling-Hammond and Goodwin 1993):

1. The work of professionals relies on a codified body of knowledge, which is not applied routinely but rather according to the individual needs of each case.
2. Entry to the profession must be strictly controlled by members within the profession through internally structured mechanisms that regulate recruitment, training, licensure, and standards for appropriate and ethical practice.
3. Professionals owe their primary responsibility to the needs of the clients; this ethical commitment should override secondary imperatives, such as personal gain, political exigencies, or simple expedience.

Professional practice is distinguished by its efforts to become client-oriented and knowledge-based (Darling-Hammond 1990a; Darling-Hammond and Goodwin 1993). Professionals aim to improve practice and enhance accountability by creating means for ensuring that practitioners will be competent and committed. Professionals undergo rigorous preparation and socialization so that the public can have high levels of confidence that professionals will behave in knowledgeable and ethical ways.

On the basis of these definitions, some Africanists (Kuntz 1994) are still of the opinion that teaching of African languages is still not quite a profession. Kuntz (1994, 4) listed the following as some of the factors contributing to the "backwardness" if the African language profession:

a. **Lack of framework**: There are no guidelines for instruction focusing on listening, speaking, reading, writing, and culture;

b. **Lack of funding**: Funding is a major limitation for African language teachers. This problem is compounded by a lack of expertise in proposal writing, competition among African Studies Centers and small enrolments which discourages departments from hiring permanent instructors for African language courses.

c. **Lack of articulation**: The failure of articulation manifests itself at several levels. Most African language instructors do not collaborate with language instructors at other institutions, with African missions, with heritage communities, or with language instructors in Africa.

d. **Lack of institutional program design**: Deficiencies in program design affect significantly the scope of research, teacher credentials, student assessment and employment expectations, language maintenance, and teacher supervision.

Missing is the fact that progress toward professionalism can be recognized by (1) the requirements for training and entry into an occupation, (2) the nature of the work and the structure of the job, (3) the authority relations that govern these things, and (4) the bases for accountability, including the relationship that exists between practitioners and their clients and between practitioners and the society at large (Darling-Hammond and Goodwin 1993).

Despite Kuntz's rather gloomy analysis of the Prospect for an African language pedagogical profession, it is crucial to note that ALTA has shown steady growth in professionalism since 1990 in each of the areas presented, and there is great promise for the field's development. In the following sections, we will describe some of the considerable progress toward profession-alism, especially in the past decade.

4. THE ROLE OF ALTA

What role has ALTA played in professionalizing the field of African language pedagogy? Since 1990, there have been many activities undertaken by ALTA members to grow a field-wide professional discipline. Some of these activities include the following initiatives.

1. Through the efforts of the national African language task forces and some support from NCOLCTL, the Swahili language field has materials such as *Swahili Teachers Manual*, Web-based materials, and video and audio materials; the Hausa language field has many computer-based materials, interactive videos, and a Hausa culture curriculum; the Yoruba language field has materials from first-year to advanced levels including videos, audio materials, CD-ROMs, and other technology-based materials for, a Yoruba font that will allow instructors and learners to write in Yoruba on he web or in email with the correct tones and diacritical marks.

2. There are Web-based materials for Intermediate Swahili, textbook development for Zulu, advanced-level CD-ROM for Yoruba, video materials, dictionaries, readers, and other pedagogical materials for learning some of the less commonly taught African languages.

3. LUGHA, the ALTA newsletter, is now published regularly on an annual basis.

4. In 1995, ALTA instituted an Award for Excellence in Leadership in the profession. Since then, many noted African language scholars have received this award.

5. Through the efforts of the ALTA board, ALTA membership has increased (both individual and institutional) and has attracted international members.

6. After many years of tagging its activities onto other national and international associations' conferences, ALTA inaugurated its own annual international conference in 1997. Pedagogists and other scholars present professional papers, choosing the ALTA conference over more established conferences such as ACAL and ASA. As a consequence of the ALTA conference, the first volume of the *Journal of African Language Teachers Association* (JALTA) was produced in the spring of 1999 and its second volume in the spring of 2000.

7. ALTA organizes annual professional development workshops, most of which take place during the annual conference to allow more members to participate. Starting in the year 2000, this workshop will be sponsored by the National African Language Resource Center (NALRC, described in section 5.3, below) which resides on the campus of the University of Wisconsin-Madison. The NALRC is also a new development in the field, another milestone toward professionalism.

8. Through the efforts of the ALTA membership, there is now a regular teacher training workshop for teaching assistants. Three African language programs in the Midwest participated in this workshop in 1998. Other Midwestern African language programs are hoping to participate in future workshops.

9. As a consequence of the success realized by some of the task forces, some were collectively able to secure fellowships at the National Foreign Language Center in Washington, DC to engage in research on curriculum matters and the incorporation of culture into the teaching of African languages.

10. Some ALTA members have published scholarly articles in reputable academic journals, reporting on research into African language learning and teaching. These include the *Modern Language Journal*, *Journal of the African Languages and Linguistics,* and *Journal of African Language Teachers Association*.

11. Members have also represented ALTA at national conferences such as the annual conference of the American Council of Teachers of Foreign Languages and the National Council of Organizations of Less Commonly Taught Languages. Members participated in these conferences as presenters and discussants.

12. The African Language Summer Cooperative Institute offered the highest number of African languages during its 1998 summer session. Many more African language programs are also participating in this collaborative effort.

The list of achievements speaks volumes for ALTA considering it life span. The two major factors that stand out in the achievements are cooperation and access. More than ever before, ALTA members are engaged in collaborative pedagogical activities and research with a clear objective: to provide a collective solution to common problems and avoid reinventing the wheel in various programs. Members are now more eager to know what their colleagues are doing and are willing to share resources. We can also say that more than ever before, ALTA members work together to provide access to the learning and teaching of African languages through materials development. Now many more traditional and nontraditional students have access to learning certain African languages, whether they are offered at their institutions or not.

5. THE NATIONAL AFRICAN LANGUAGE RESOURCE CENTER

The National African Language Resource Center (NALRC) is a tri-annually and federally-funded, nonprofit, national foreign language center dedicated to the advancement of African language teaching and learning in the United States. It was inaugurated in the spring of 1999 after receiving a major grant from the U.S. Department of Education. The Center's mission is to serve the entire community of African language educators and students in the United States by sponsoring a wide range of educational and professional activities designed to improve the accessibility and quality of African language instruction in the United States. The Center encourages a variety of pedagogical approaches to accommodate learner diversity. It advocates the integration of language and culture learning and the development of fluency in these areas. It facilitates dialogue among teachers, learners, and administrators from a wide variety of cultural and institutional perspectives and promotes the profession of African language teaching.

The concept of NALRC offers a fundamentally new approach to African language programming in the United States. It will address concerns of all sectors (traditional and non-traditional students); Americans and particularly, Americans of African descent who are interested in African languages and cultures; and high school and grade school teachers who are interested in introducing African languages and cultures into their curricula. NALRC does so from a truly national perspective. But most importantly, it has as its purpose and primary agenda the development of the teaching and learning of African languages in this country using the full expertise of the African language pedagogists throughout this nation and not at a single academic institution. More specifically, the Center:

- provides a national training facility for teachers and program-mers (faculty and graduate assistants) of African languages;
- provides fellowships for faculty and graduate students to develop their careers African language programming;
- collects and disseminates information specifically concerning African languages;
- provides support for specific development projects which will facilitate the learning of African languages:
- conducts basic research on the teaching and learning of African languages and undertakes the structural analysis of under-documented African languages so that better learning materials can be constructed;
- designs African language programs, curricula, and materials and links them with study abroad programs, providing for their effective management (this process is one of developing a national consensus and as a consequence one of developing national standards);
- develops materials for the learning of African languages based on basic linguistic research, on current pedagogical practices, and in consort with potential users of the materials;

- develops effective means for the evaluation and assessment of programs, curricula, courses, and learner achievement;
- provided infrastructural support for the field of African languages through the support of the work of ALTA's Language Learning Framework Task Forces.

In addition, we anticipate that the results of new NALRC research focused on the learning of African languages will raise new theoretical issues about second language acquisition that can only make the field more vital.

5.1 The NALRC Compared with Existing LRCs

What is the functional difference between NALRC and other National Language Resource Centers (LRCs)? NALRC has a singular mission of promoting access to the learning of African languages in the United States. With its national focus, the Center is also national in design. This is because it draws on the available expertise in America and elsewhere, regardless of location. This has been accomplished by making the Center "virtual," with administrative staff located in one place, but with provisions for incorporating national and international expertise else where. This design facilitates a wide range of national and international networking activities as called for by the legislation. Furthermore, the Center not only develops classroom materials, technology, techniques and strategies for developing proficiency in African languages, but it also seeks to develop program designs which match classroom content with a wide variety of learner needs including scholars and heritage learners as well as the commercial and service sectors. It also assesses national needs in African languages (which languages to offer, what kinds of classes and at what levels) from a national perspective and, as a result, develops programs to meet those needs. And finally, the Center serves as a focal point for bringing together those with interests in language learning, from basic research and language acquisition to the teaching and learning of specific languages.

5.2 The Role of NALRC

The role of NALRC in the professionalization of the field is to strengthen research, teaching, and learning of African languages. To meet this objective, the Center focuses on projects that encourage:

1. learner accessibility to as many African languages as possible;
2. collaboration with foreign language educators and professional associations;
3. development and coordination of networking frameworks and activities;
4. overseas and domestic African language summer institutes.

The Center is a truly *national* resource center, not only in its organization and structure but also in the way the Center's activities and projects reflect national needs and interests. The results of its projects will be disseminated nationally through innovative uses of technology, journals, publications, workshops, and consultancy programs that the Center will establish.

5.3 NALRC Project Areas

The projects proposed in the following five categories address problems facing the field of African language learning and teaching nationwide and seek to find long-term solutions to common problems.

NATIONAL COORDINATION PROJECT

Projects in this category are designed to investigate and assess the national needs for African language offerings since it is not possible to teach the more than 1,000 of African languages. This includes projects that identify material needs for African languages and generate a prioritized list, result in the development of an inventory of African language programs in the United States, and focus on the collection of data concerning the history of African Languages in the United States. Below are examples of projects and activities undertaken by NALRC:

Assessing Current National Needs for African Languages: The field of African language pedagogy needs to gain a clearer idea of what the national needs are with respect to African languages. This project will be led by an ALTA professional with extensive expertise in African language programming in the United States (Dwyer 1999). The project will call for a meeting of African language coordinators, center directors, and national language planners to meet for a weekend to develop a plan that can be used to assess African language needs and availability in the U.S. The result of this assessment will guide future projects on needs and assessment.

African Language Materials Needs, a Prioritized List: Teachers and specialists will be surveyed for the purpose of identifying specific materials needs for each of the highest-priority African languages (Wiley and Dwyer, 1980, designated 82 African languages as priority languages for instruction and material development). The results will be integrated into a master list and then published on the Web for a maximum distribution.

An Inventory of African Language Programs in the United States: There is a need for a common format for describing language offerings in the United States. While a list of available African language courses is being managed by CARLA at the University of Minnesota, a compatible list of programs would be useful to students, language planners, and others.

A Data History of African Languages in the United States: A collection of data dating back to at least 1970 shows (a) African language programs, (b) language offerings; (c) faculty; (d) enrollments figures by institution; follow-up on students (especially FLAS recipients); (e) summer institutes and Group Projects Abroad; and (f) projects undertaken by ALTA members. As time passes, much of this data may become irretrievably lost. ALTA, the Association of African Studies Programs, and the U.S. Department of Education need this information for African languages promotions and for categorizing languages.

Clearinghouse for Out-of-Print African Language Learning Materials: Many of useful African language learning materials are out of print, difficult for teachers and learners to access. A way to make such materials available to language learners is needed. This would involve obtaining permission for reproducing the materials and determining how to disseminate them. For example, they could be scanned and digitized and made available on the Web or on CD-ROM disc. They could also be photocopied. This project will follow the recommendations of the Center and will, where possible, make these materials more accessible.

PERSONNEL DEVELOPMENT PROJECTS

This area includes (a) specialized training and development of new faculty members (language coordinators); (b) continued training and professional development of existing faculty members; and (c) the ongoing training and development of teaching assistants. The goal of these projects to give African language instructors the training needed to ensure quality instruction in African language programs. Issues of certification and standardization will also be addressed in these projects. The Center will undertake the following projects and activities for personnel development:

Training African Language Supertrainers: Supertrainers are seasoned language professionals who can provide top notch training to current and new teachers in the field. Three or four teachers (preferably full-time faculty members) will be trained as supertrainers. They will then train other African language teachers. The need for full-time faculty members is critical in the selection of supertrainers to allow for continuity. This week-long training will give African language instructors the opportunity to increase their expertise in incorporating current research on language learning into their classroom instruction.

A Week-long Training Program for African Language TAs: Most of the teaching assistants employed in African language programs are native speakers of their respective African languages who may or may not have taught their language to first-language speakers. Most are graduate students with no experience in teaching their languages to non-native speakers. The only experience some of these graduate students have is speaking the language. These assistants need exposure to the design, goals, and methodology of the teaching of African languages to non-native speakers, particularly in the United States. The Center plans to make the training of such individuals an annual event for teaching assistants.

Summer Institute Professionalizing Training: This program is designed to increase the expertise of the African language faculty by focusing on a specific area such as teacher training, program development, direction and evaluation, curriculum development and assessment, materials development and evaluation, computer-assisted language learning, course design, proficiency assessment, integration of culture into classroom activities, the use of authentic language even in first year language courses, goal-driven curriculum, or a content-based approach to language instruction. The Center will offer this training session to ten participants per year.

One-Semester Faculty Residential Fellowship: One fellowship will be awarded each year, on a competitive basis, for an African language faculty member to pursue additional training in teaching methodology, teacher training, program design, and evaluation, national language planning, computer-assisted language learning, or for the development of a specific project. The fellow will be hosted at the NALRC offices in Madision.

Doctoral Fellowship: Training New Professionals: To increase the expertise of new language coordinators, a one-year fellowship will be awarded on a competitive basis to a (potential) teacher of an African language to receive specialized training in teaching methodology, teacher training, program design and evaluation, national language planning, and computer-assisted language training. The fellowship year will be spent at the Center.

A Day-Long Training Session at the Annual ALTA Conference: For continued professionalization of African language teachers, new perspectives and approaches need to be introduced at the annual meeting at which 30 to 40 African language teachers typically gather. The training session will include topics such as new software, how to avoid using English in a foreign language classroom, culture, the first-year syllabus, integrating video, using audio texts, program design and evaluation. This will also become an annual event.

PROGRAM DEVELOPMENT AND EVALUATION PROJECTS

In this project area, issues of national integration (need and standardization), faculty status, program design, language assessment, and program purpose will all be addressed. Below are some of the activities on which the Center will focus.

Evaluating African Language Programs Workshop: This three-day workshop will work toward the development of a set of categories for African language programs which include a consideration of program goals (number and types), the training of personnel, types of courses and sample syllabi, course design, and the measurement of learners' outcomes. Each program will be asked to describe its language program in these terms for a publication that will appear at a common web site. This project is needed because learners, teachers, and administrators have a need to know what each African language program offers with respect to the suggested categories for any number of reasons. About ten participants will participate in this project . Each participant will represent a different African language program.

Developing Guidelines for the Evaluation of Programs: Almost every African language program in the United States has undergone by an external review; however, there is currently no uniform method of review. This project will bring program reviewers and those whose programs have been reviewed together to identify aspects of reviews that are truly useful in understanding how a program operates. This project will publish guidelines for evaluating African language programs in the United States.

Identifying National Needs, Types of Study, and Specific Languages and Integrating Them with Institutional Resources: A priority listing for African language materials needs has not been done in the last 20 years. Since then, new textual and multimedia materials have been developed and the growing national need has yet to be considered. This one-week project will develop ways to gather field-wide input into the language priorities within each African language and the types of materials that are needed.

RESEARCH PROJECTS

The majority of those who currently teach African languages teach the language on the side but do their own research in fields other than language pedagogy. As a result, most do not see the teaching of African languages as a priority. The NALRC provides a means to actively encourage African language instructors to engage in research on African languages. It is important to see how current research and methodologies apply to the teaching of African languages. Below is a list of topics that the Center will address.

The Acquisition of Tones in African Languages: Almost 90% of the languages spoken in Africa are tonal. Tonal languages sometimes create problems for foreigners who are familiar only with stress-type languages. This research will help to identify the processes through which foreigners, particularly American learners, acquire tones in languages such as Akan, Kikuyu, Ndebele, Shona, Zulu, Twi, and Yoruba. Identifying problems or successes in acquiring tones can inform the field of how African tonal languages should be taught.

The Communicative Orientation of African Language Textbooks: Canale and Swain's (1980) and other recent works in second and foreign language acquisition suggest that communicative competence consists of four major components: grammatical competence, sociolinguistic competence, discourse competence, and strategic competence. Some scholars also believe that communicative competence—knowledge of the language— must be considered separately from communicative performance (skill in using the language in different contexts with varying degrees of accuracy) and to achieve a variety of goals using different language functions. Many African language teachers now seek to redesign their African language courses—and the instructional materials they use—to reflect the growing recognition that the development of grammatical competence is but one part of the larger task of the development of communicative competence.

This project will examine the notion of a communicatively oriented textbook; establish criteria for the evaluation of the communicative orientation of African language textbooks; evaluate the communicative orientation of some of the most popular four-skill introductory, intermediate, and advanced African language textbooks.

A Review of Computer-Assisted Language Learning Software for African Languages: The continued improvements of technology and the ever-falling prices of hardware have made personal computers a viable educational tool. Foreign language specialists have taken advantage of new computer technologies and has been producing CALL software. In comparison with other languages, only a handful of people have been working on CALL software for African languages (largely because of a lack of funds), and even fewer of them have made their products commercially available. The purposes of this project are to provide the public with a brief history of CALL for African languages and also to introduce some of the CALL software for African languages that is available to the general public in the U.S. in the form of commercial products or as shareware.

Learner Strategies and Management for African Languages: Recent developments have placed increased emphasis on the role of the learner in language acquisition. This is especially true in

African languages since teachers have fewer opportunities for training and professional development. A greater understanding of how learners currently manage their acquisition of an African language would not only help African language classes; it would provide important insights into second language acquisition as well. Of special interest are seeking learner-defined goals for African languages, developing self-assessment techniques, and identifying successful study techniques.

Toward Cultural Proficiency in African Languages: In the last three decades, there has been a great interest in increasing the cultural content of the foreign language curriculum. This is reflected in the large body of foreign language literature on the study of target cultures and relevance to language teaching.

Interest in the communicative- and proficiency-based approaches to foreign language teaching in the '80s and the '90s has also given the teaching of culture a boost. Galloway (1981) notes that "the ability to communicate in another language requires not only knowledge of the grammatical system of a language, but also knowledge of the patterns of living, acting, reacting, seeing, and explaining the world of the target country as well." Omaggio-Hadley (1993) also state that the teaching of culture both as a topic in its own right and as it is embedded in language use is an important aspect of language teaching that is oriented toward communicative proficiency. Therefore, "the study of culture must be integrated with the study of language if students are to derive lasting benefits from their language learning experience" (Omaggio-Hadley 1993).

The importance of culture in foreign language proficiency was also revealed by the inclusion of culture in the *ACTFL Provisional Proficiency Guidelines* of 1984. The section on culture was the least developed, and it was therefore dropped in the revised form in 1986. There is no doubt that it is difficult to teach culture. Crawford-Lange and Lange (1984) also pointed out that one of the problems with teaching culture in foreign language classrooms is that many language teachers feel that their knowledge of the target language is inadequate because of limited exposure to the culture. In addition, familiarity with the culture does not imply the ability to integrate the teaching of culture into language teaching. For these reasons, culture poses a strong challenge to many foreign language teachers. Multimedia technology, however, has made it easier today for teachers to incorporate culture into language teaching.

This crucial project will result in designing an evaluation framework to evaluate cultural information in first year textbooks for Bambara, Chichewa, Fula, Hausa, Igbo, Kanuri, Kikuyu, Kirundi, Lingala, Luganda, Ndebele, Sango, Shona, Swahili, Wolof, Xhosa, Yoruba, and Zulu. The research will present a model of how cultural information can be successfully integrated into textbooks. The results of this research will influence the way cultural information will be presented in future African language textbooks and will also influence how languages are taught in the classrooms.

MATERIALS DEVELOPMENT AND DISSEMINATION PROJECTS

Materials development is one of the biggest problems facing African language teaching and learning in the United States. The majority of the African languages taught in the U.S. do not have textbook materials that incorporate current research into foreign language pedagogy. One of the goals of the NALRC is to be able to sponsor projects that will result in the emergence of teaching and learning materials for priority African languages. The Center will ensure that materials will incorporate current research on the teaching and learning of foreign languages. The Center will also ensure that those materials will be disseminated nationally by assisting textbook writers to publish their works through the NALRC. The Center will also pay close attention to what is being developed and then make the works available.

Technology materials development for a particular African language that can easily serve as a model for other African languages is given preference in the competition for materials development funding through the Center. Model textbook development is also given a high priority to make projects cost-efficient. Below is a list of materials to be developed from the ALTA wish list:

A CD-ROM Template for African Language Learning: With funds from the U.S. Department of Education, Antonia Folarin-Schleicher has developed a CD-ROM template for elementary and intermediate Yoruba language levels. This Yoruba CD-ROM template was developed not only to help Yoruba learners and instructors in the language learning and teaching processes, but also to serve as a template for other foreign language learners and instructors.

One of the goals of the NALRC is to make this template available to other African language instructors so that they can use it to develop similar CD-ROMs for languages such as Hausa, Swahili, Zulu, Shona, Wolof, and Lingala. Availability of the template will make similar projects more cost-effective and can save developers time. Other materials development projects that may be done at the NALRC include:

1.   A first-year CD-ROM template for an African language;
2.   A guide to Web-based multimedia resources for African languages;
3.   A guide for using African language resource materials;
4.   A model first-year course in an African language;
5.   A model second-year course in an African language;
6.   A Yoruba-English, English-Yoruba Dictionary;
7.   A reference grammar for Yoruba;
8.   A Kiswahili Web site;
9.   An advanced Kiswahili learners manual ;
10. K-12 Kiswahili learning materials;
11. A subject-based dictionary in Kiswahili;
12. A traveler's introduction to Hausa language and culture;
13. A guide to Yoruba oral proficiency evaluation;
14. Xhosa-English English-Xhosa Dictionary;
15. A hypertext cultural reader for Zulu;
16. An interactive Wolof course ;
17. An Akan-English English-Akan Dictionary;
18. Video texts for beginning and intermediate Fula. This suggests the kinds of materials that the Center will support on a competitive and national needs basis.

Scholarship and the Professionalization of African Language Pedagogy

The role of scholarship in professionalizing African language pedagogy is important to us. If we look at all of the ALTA and NALRC activities listed above, it is clear that scholarship is at their heart. It is at the heart of any academic discipline or profession. But what the African language teaching profession has not addressed thus far is what we mean by scholarship in African language learning and teaching. If our goal, as pointed out by Dwyer (1995) and Eyamba (1996), is to foster the scholarship of African language learning and teaching, then as an ALTA body, we need to revisit what we mean by scholarship. What does it mean to be an African language scholar?

One should not be regarded as an African language scholar only after having published a paper on Hausa, Swahili, or Yoruba phonology or phonetics. Neither should one be regarded as an African language scholar only after having published a paper on literary analysis of a Swahili, Hausa, or Yoruba poem or novel. The term scholar should include those whose expertise is in language pedagogy. Expertise in second language acquisition in African languages which involves research on how adults learn African languages is part of the definition of an African language scholar.

Ernest Boyer (1995), defines a scholar as someone who engages in original research (in any field), someone who can step back from his or her investigation and look for connections with other disciplines, someone who can build bridges between theory and practice, and someone who can communicate one's knowledge effectively to others through teaching. Scholarly activities relies on a base of expertise, a "scholarly knowing" that needs to and can be identified, made public, and evaluated; a scholarship that faculty themselves must be responsible for monitoring.

He sees the work of a scholar as having four separate but overlapping functions:

1. Scholarship of Discovery (finding out what is yet to be designated specialized research);
2. Scholarship of Integration (making connection between disciplines, multi-disciplinary);

3. Scholarship of Application (participating in service activities that are tied directly to one's special field of knowledge and relate to and flow directly out of this professional activity consulting; linking theory and practice);

4. Scholarship of Teaching (communicating the knowledge discovered effectively. When teaching is defined as scholarship, it both educates and entices future scholars. Aristotle said "Teaching is the highest form of understanding").

According to Boyer (1995), every aspect of these functions marks a scholar. And when we take stock of all the professional activities that many ALTA members have engaged in to-date, it is clear that we do not only have African language scholars in our field, we also have emerging scholars in the field of African language learning and teaching whose scholarship we need to recognize, acknowledge, and reward. All the activities listed above fit into one function of scholarship or the other as argued by Boyer (1995).

The problem of recognition does not lie with the field but rather with the academy. What we urgently need, therefore, is an academy with more inclusive views of what it means to be a scholar, i.e., a recognition that knowledge is acquired or discovered not only through research—finding what has not been found before—it is also acquired through synthesis (looking for connection between what has been found and other fields of studies), through practice applying what has been found to real life situations (e.g., consulting, service that relates directly to one's field of studies), and through teaching (ability to communicate effectively the knowledge we found, and ability to document our teaching so that it can be made public and others can evaluate it).

All these functions of a scholar are various academic work which dynamically interact and forms an interdependent whole. This kind of vision of scholarship, i.e., one that recognizes, acknowledges and *rewards* the great diversity of talent in the field of African language pedagogy, will especially be useful to all members as they reflect on the meaning and direction of their professional lives. It will also help to encourage many in the field in fostering the scholarship of the teaching of African languages.

To conclude this section, a profession is formed when members of an occupation agree that they have a knowledge base, that what they know relates directly to effective practice, that being prepared is essential to being a responsible practitioner.

6. CONCLUSION

ALTA as a voice of authority for the field can energize the field to feel good about itself , make members work towards a common goal which is to make the field a recognized and competitive professional field. For the last eight years, ALTA has succeeded in organizing and coordinating its field-wide development through planning and networking. It is time for ALTA to be the national voice to institutions, policy makers and funders, articulate the needs (including the priorities of these needs) in maintaining and pushing the field further ahead in its development.

The ability for ALTA to coordinate the capacity of the field to produce materials that reflect shared needs will ensure a field-wide collaborative effort to collect data and to plan efficiently, to benefit all languages especially those which still lag behind in many respects. It will continue to be the avenue through which the field, collectively, address skills and levels in a range of shared concerns from the field.

Last but not least, ALTA should take a front row position in establishing sustainable relationship with the countries of the languages being taught in the United States and other parts of the world. These home countries are the critical sources of expertise, teachers, instructional materials, and other resources that are necessary to develop the field, materials and programs. ALTA needs to establish a strong infrastructure capable of facilitating the flow of expertise, teachers, materials, mechanisms for scholarly exchange in the language area, faculty/student exchange programs, study abroad programs, and cross-country collaborative projects. Most of all, ALTA needs to be a real voice for the field, a voice that can impact even those institutions which still relegate Africa to a footnote in its general curriculum and consequently render the African language instruction a low priority.

APPENDIX: THE SURVEY QUESTIONS

The following questions were sent to different African language coordinators.

1. What percentage of graduate and undergraduate students study African languages?
2. Which African languages have you offered over the past years during the academic year?
3. Which African languages have you offered during the summer over the past five years?
4. Who coordinates your African language program? What percentage of this person's appointment is allocated for this purpose?
5. List the names of your African language faculty and indicate what percentage of this person's appointment is allocated to the teaching of African languages?
6. If you regularly employ Teaching Assistants to teach your African language courses, indicate what minimal qualifications such individuals are expected to have in the areas of language proficiency, field of specialization and degree of language teaching training.
7. Do you have a degree program in African languages?

BIBLIOGRAPHY

Alao, George. 2000. "African Languages Abroad: Problems and Proposals." *Journal of the African Language Teachers Association* 1:63-83.

Al-Batal, Mahmoud. 1988. "Towards Cultural Proficiency in Arabic." *Foreign Language Annals* 5:443-448.

Alessi, Stephen M. and Stanley R. Trollip. 1991. *Computer-Based Instruction: Methods and Development.* Englewood Cliffs, NJ: Prentice Hall.

Allan, M. 1985. *Teaching English with Video.* Harlow, England: Longman.

Allen, Wendy W. 1985. "Toward Cultural Proficiency." In *Proficiency, Curriculum, Articulation: The Ties that Bind,* ed. Alice C. Omaggio. Middlebury, VT: Northeast Conference, 137-66.

———— and Keith Anderson. 1994. Languages Across the Curriculum: An Agenda. In Straight, H. Stephen. (ed.). *Languages Across the Curriculum: Translation Perspectives VII.* Center for Research in Translation, State University of New York at Binghamton.

————, K. Anderson, and L. Narvaez. 1992. "Foreign Languages Across the Curriculum: The Applied Foreign Language Component." *Foreign Language Annals* 25:11-19.

Bibliography

Anderson, Keith, Wendy Allen, and Leon Narvaez. 1993. "The Applied Foreign Language Component in the Humanities and the Sciences." In *Language and Content: Discipline- and Content-Based Approaches to Language Study,* ed. M. Krueger and F. Ryan. Lexington, MA: D. C. Heath, 103-113.

Arasanyin, Frank O., Antonia Y. Folarin-Schleicher, and R. Sekoni. 1996. "A Goal-Driven Curriculum." Unpublished manuscript. Washington, D.C.: National Foreign Language Center, Johns Hopkins University.

Barber, Karen. 1985. *Yoruba Dun Un So: A Beginner's Course in Yoruba.* New Haven, CT: Yale UP.

Beauvois, Margaret H. 1997. "Computer-Mediated Communication (CMC): Technology for Improving Speaking and Writing." In *Technology Enhanced Language Learning,* ed. Michael D. Bush and Robert M. Terry. Lincolnwood, IL: National Textbook Company.

Becker H. S. 1962. "The Nature of a Profession." In *Education for the Professions: The Sixty-First Yearbook of the National Society for the Study of Education,* ed. N. B. Henry. Chicago: U of Chicago P, 27-46.

Bennett, Patrick K., et al. 1985. *A First Course in Kikuyu.* Madison: African Studies Program, University of Wisconsin.

———., et al. 1985. *An Introduction to Kikuyu Conversation.* Madison: African Studies Program, University of Wisconsin.

Bokamba, Eyamba. 1996. "African Language Instruction in the 21st Century: Current Realities and Future Visions." Paper presented at the ALTA Parasession, University of Florida, Gainesville.

Boyer, Earnest. 1995. *Scholarship Reconsidered: Priorities of the Professorate.* Princeton, NJ: Carnegie Foundation for the Advancement of Teaching.

216

Brecht, Richard D. and Ronald Walton. 1995. "The Future Shape of Language Learning in the New World of Global Communications: Consequences for Higher Education and Beyond." In *Foreign Language Learning: The Journey of a Lifetime,* ed. Richard Donato and Robert Terry. Lincolnwood, IL: National Textbook Company, 110-152.

Brecht, Richard D. and Ronald Walton. 1994. *National Strategic Planning in the Less Commonly Taught Languages.* Washington, D.C.: National Foreign Language Center.

Brinton, D. M., Marguerite A. Snow, and Marjorie B. Wesche. 1989. *Content-Based Second Language Instruction.* New York: Newbury.

Brooks, Nelson. 1968. "Teaching Culture in the Foreign Language Classroom." *Foreign Language Annals* 1:204-17.

———. 1971. "Culture: A New Frontier." *Foreign Language Annals* 5:54-61.

Brown, G. and Yule, G. 1983. *Teaching, the Spoken Language.* Cambridge: Cambridge UP.

Burger, S. 1989. "Content-Based ESL in a Sheltered Psychology Course: Input, Output, and Outcomes." *TESL Canada Journal* 6(2):45-59.

Canale, Michael and Merrill Swain. 1980. "Theoretical Bases of Communicative Approaches to Second Language Teaching and Testing." *Applied Linguistics* 1:1-47.

Cantoni-Harvey, G. 1987. *Content-Area Language Instruction: Approaches and Strategies.* Reading, MA: Addison-Wesley.

Center for Critical Thinking. 1996. "Defining Critical Thinking." http://www.sonoma.edu/cthink/University/univclass/D-efining.nclk. Sonoma, CA: Sonoma State University.

Chaffee, J. 1988. *Thinking Critically,* 2nd ed. Boston: Houghton Mifflin.

Chamot, A. U. 1990. "Cognitive Instruction in the Second Language Classroom: The Role of Learning Strategies." *Georgetown University Roundtable on Languages and Linguistics,* 496-513.

Clément, R. and B. G. Kruidenier. 1985. "Aptitude, Attitude and Motivation in Second Language Proficiency: A Test of Clément's Model." *Journal of Language and Social Psychology* 4:21-37.

Clément, R., Z. Dornyei, and K. A. Noels. 1994. "Motivation, Self-Confidence, and Group Cohesion in the Foreign Language Classroom." *Language Learning* 44:417-448.

Clément, R., R. C. Gardner, and P. C. Smythe. 1977. "Motivational Variables in Second Language Acquisition: A Study of Francophones Learning English." *Canadian Journal of Behavioral Science* 12:123-133.

————. 1980. "Social and Individual Factors in Second Language Acquisition. *Canadianjjournal of Behavioral Science* 12:293-302.

Cowan, Ronayne and Russell G. Schuh. 1976. *Spoken Hausa.* Ithaca, NY: Spoken Language Series.

Crandall, Jodi, ed. 1987. *ESL through Content-Area Instruction: Mathematics, Science, Social Studies.* Englewood Cliffs, NJ: Prentice-Hall.

Crawford-Lange, Linda, and Dale Lange. 1984. Doing the Unthinkable in the Second-Language Classroom. In T. Higgs, ed., *Teaching for Proficiency, The Organizing Principle.* ACTFL Foreign Language Education Series, vol. 15. Lincolnwood, IL: National Textbook Company.

Cyffer, Norbert. 1991. *We Learn Kanuri.* Köln, Germany: Rüdiger Koppe.

D'Angelo, E. 1971. *The Teaching of Critical thinking.* Amsterdam: B.R. Gruner.

Bibliography

Darling-Hammond, L. 1990. "Teacher Professionalism: Why and How?" In *Schools as Collaborative Cultures: Creating the Future Now*, ed. A. Lieberman. New York: Falmer, 25-50.

Drake, S. 1993. "Planning Integrated Curricula." *The Call for Adventure*. Alexandria, VA: ASCD.

Dwyer, David. 1991. *Final Report of the Conference on African Language-Teaching in the US: Directions for the 1990s.* East Lansing, MI: Kellogg Center.

————. 1995. "African Language Teachers Association: Future Directions of ALTA Field Development." *NCOLCTL Bulletin* 1(2): 7-8.

————. 1999a. "Developing a Language Learning Rationale for African Language Tutorials. " *Journal of the African Language Teachers Association* 1:115-134.

————. 1999b. "The Future of African Language Programming in the United States: The Concept of a National African Language Center." *Journal of the African Language Teachers Association* 1:1-24.

———— and Lioba Moshi. 1994. *The Field of Academic African Language Programming.* Unpublished manuscript.

———— and Wiley David 1981. *Directions and Priority for the 1980's.* Michigan State University, African Studies Center.

————, Lioba Moshi, and Antonia Schleicher. 1999. "The Role of Culture in the Language Classroom." *Journal of the African Language Teachers Association* 1:85-113.

ELT Documents. 1979. *The Use of the Media in English Language Teaching.* London: British Council.

Folarin-Schleicher, Antonia Y. 1993. *Je K'A So Yoruba.* New Haven, CT: Yale UP.

Fortune, George. 1967. *Elements of Shona.* London: Longman.

Galloway, Vicki B. 1981. *Communicating in a Cultural Context: The Global Perspective*. Proceedings of the 1981 Summer Cross-Cultural Workshop for Foreign Language Teachers. Columbia, SC: South Carolina State Department of Education.

Gardner, R. C. 1985. *Social Psychology and Second Language Learning: The Role of Attitudes and Motivation*. London: Edward Arnold.

———— and W. E. Lambert. 1959. "Motivational Variables in Second Language Acquisition." *Canadian Journal of Psychology* 13:226-272.

Geddes, M. and G. Sturtridge, eds. 1982. *Video in the Language Classroom*. London: Heinemann.

Goodlad, J. I. 1990. *Teachers for Our Nation's Schools*. San Francisco: Jossey-Bass.

Hall, Edward T. 1859. *The Silent Language*. Greenwich, CT: Fawcett.

Hinnebusch, Thomas J. and Sarah M. Mirza. 1998. *Kiswahili Msingi wa Kusema, Kusoma, na Kuandika*. New York: United P of America

Hutchison, John and Mamadou Kante. 1977. *Introductory Bambara*. Bloomington: Indiana U African Studies Center.

Jackson, William K. and Tricia Kalivoda. 1997. *Teaching at UGA* 15(2):1-2.

Joiner, Elizabeth. 1997. "Teaching Listening: How Technology Can Help." In *Technology Enhanced Language Learning*, ed. Michael D. Bush and Robert M. Terry. Lincolnwood, IL: National Textbook Company, 77-120.

Jones, Jermaine, ed. *Aroko Awon Akeko Yoruba Olodun Kiini Si Iketa*. Unpublished manuscript. African Studies Program, University of Wisconsin.

Jurasek, Richard. 1982. "Practical Applications of Foreign Languages in the College Curriculum." *Modern Language Journal* 66:368-72.

———. 1988. "Integrating Foreign Languages into the College Curriculum." *Modern Language Journal* 72:52-58.

———. 1992. "Languages Across the Curriculum: A Case History from Earlham College and a Generic Rationale." In *Language and Content: Discipline- and Content-Based Approa-ches to Language Study,* ed. M. Krueger and F. Ryan. Lexington, MA: D. C. Heath, 85-102.

———. 1994. "Languages Across the Curriculum Across the Country." In *Languages Across the Curriculum: Translation Perspectives VII,* ed. H. Stephen. Binghamton: Center for Research in Translation, State U of New York.

Kamoga, F. Katabazi and Earl W. Stevick. 1968. *Luganda Basic Course.* Washington, D.C.: Foreign Language Institute.

Kimble, G. and N. Garmezy. 1963. *Principles of General Psychology,* 2nd ed. New York: Ronald Press.

King, Charlotte P. 1990. "A Linguistic and a Cultural Competence: Can They Live Happily Together?" *Foreign Language Annals* 1:65-70.

Klee, Carol A. and Michael F. Metcalf. 1994. "Perspectives on Foreign Languages Across the Curriculum Based on the University of Minnesota Experience." In *Languages Across the Curriculum: Translation Perspectives VII,* ed. H. Stephen Straight. Binghamton: Center for Research in Translation, State U of New York.

Kraft, C. H. and A. H. M. Kirk-Greene. 1973. *Teach Yourself Hausa.* Dunton Green, UK: Hodder and Stoughton.

Kramsch, Claire. 1988a. "Beyond the Skill vs. Content Debate: The Multiple Discourse Worlds of the Foreign Language Curriculum." In *Language Learning and Liberal Education*, ed. Peter C. Patrikis. New Haven, CT: Consortium for Language Teaching and Learning.

———. 1988b. "The Cultural Discourse of Foreign Language Textbooks." In *Toward a New Integration of Language and Culture*, ed. Alan Singerman. Middlebury, VT: Northeast Conference.

———. 1993. *Context and Culture in Language Teaching*, Oxford: Oxford UP.

Krashen, Stephen D. 1985a. *The Input Hypothesis: Issues and Implications*. London: Longman.

———. 1985b. *Input in Second Language Acquisition*. Oxford: Pergamon.

———. 1989. *Language Acquisition and Language Education: Extensions and Applications*. New York: Prentice Hall.

Kuntz, Patricia. 1994. "The Professionalization of African Language Instructors: Priorities for This Decade." Paper presented at the Less Commonly Taught Language Symposium, University of Illinois, Champaign-Urbana, IL.

Lafayette, Robert C. 1978. *Teaching Culture: Strategies and Techniques*. Language in Education: Theory and Practice Series no. 11. Washington, D.C.: Center for Applied Linguistics.

——— and Renate A. Schulz. 1975. "Evaluating Cultural Learning." In *Cultural Revolution in Foreign Languages: A Guide for Building the Modern Curriculum*, ed. Robert C. Lafayette. Lincolnwood, IL: National Textbook Company.

Lasebikan, E. L. 1958. *Learning Yoruba* London: Oxford UP.

Leaver, Betty Lou, Stephen B. Stryker. 1989. "Content-Based Instruction for Foreign Language Classrooms." *Foreign Language Annals* 22:269-75.

Levno, Arley W. 1980. "An Analysis of Surface Culture and Its Manner of Presentation in First-Year College French Textbooks from 1972 to 1978." *Foreign Language Annals* 1:47-52.

Little, Greta D. and Sara L. Sanders. 1989. "Classroom Community: A Prerequisite for Communication." *Foreign Language Annals* 22(3):277-81.

Lonegran, Jack. 1984. *Video in Language Teaching.* Cambridge: Cambridge UP.

Malcolm, D. 1949. *A Zulu Manual for Beginners.* London: Longman, Green, and Co.

Martínez-Lage, Ana. 1997. "Hypermedia Technology for Teaching Reading." In *Technology Enhanced Language Learning,* ed. Michael D. Bush and Robert M. Terry. Lincolnwood, IL: National Textbook Company, 121-163.

Mayr, F. 1904. *Zulu Simplified: A New Practical and Easy Method of Learning the Zulu Language.* Pietermaritzburg, South Africa: P. Davis and Sons.

Met, M. 1991. "Learning Language through Content: Learning Content through Language." *Foreign Language Annals* 75(4):281-95.

Moshi, Lioba. 1988. "Tuimarishe Kiswahili Chetu" ["Building Proficiency in Kiswahili"]. *A Textbook for Second and Third Year Students.* Lanham MD: UP of America.

———. 1992. "A Successful Language Teacher." *Teaching Ideas and Resources for African Languages* 9:36-37.

———. 1994. "The Teaching of African Languages." *Penn Language News* (Spring):1-6.

————. 1996a. *Kiswahili: Lugha na Utamaduni* (A 23-Lesson Video Series). Athens: U of Georgia Office of Instructional Support and Development.

————. 1996b. *Waswahili: Lugha, Desturi na Utamaduni* (A 7-Part Video Series). Athens: U of Georgia Office of Instructional Support and Development.

————. 1998. *Kiswahili: Lugha na Utamaduni.* Hyattsville, MD: Dunwood.

————. 1999. "The Implementation of the Language Learning Framework: The Case of Materials Development in Less Commonly Taught Languages." *Journal of the African Language Teachers Association* 1(1):155-168.

————. 2000. "The Field of African Languages: Perspectives for The 21st Century." *Journal of the African Language Teachers Association* 1(2):1-11.

———— and Ojo A. Akinloye. 2000. "A Centered WebCT Instruction for African Languages." *Journal of the African Language Teachers Association* 1(2):31-57.

————, Abdul Nanji, Magdalena Hauner, and John Mtembezi Inniss. 1999. *Mwalimu wa Kiswahili: A Language Teaching.* An ALTA Publication. Binghamton, NY: Global Publications.

Mugane John. 1999. *Tujifunze Kiswahili* [*Let's Learn Kiswahili*]. Athens, OH: Aramati Digital Technologies.

Northedge, A. 1983. *How to Study.* NC: Milton Keynes.

Nostrand, Howard L. 1967. "The Emergent Model in *Background for the Teaching of French.*" Washington, D.C.: Office of Education.

————. 1974. "Empathy for a Second Culture." In *Responding to New Realities,* ed. Gilbert Jarvis. Lincolnwood, IL: National Textbook Company, 263-327.

Nyembezi, C. and L. Sibusiso. 1957. *Learn Zulu.* Pietermaritzburg, South Africa: Shuter and Shooter.

Odujinrin, J. S. A. 1964. *Modern Lessons in Yoruba,* parts I and II. London: Waterloo.

Ojo, Akinloye and Justin Spence. 1996. "Learning Yoruba As a Second Language: A Teacher-Student Perspective." Unpublished manuscript.

Omaggio-Hadley, Alice C. 1993. *Teaching Language in Context, Proficiency-Oriented Instruction.* Boston, MA: Heinle & Heinle.

Orr, Gregory John and Carol Myers Scotton. 1980. *Learning Chichewa: Book 1. A Peace Corps Language Course.* East Lansing: African Studies Center, Michigan State U.

Owen, D. and Dunton M. 1982. *The Complete Handbook of Video.* Harmondsworth: Penguin.

Oxford, R. L. 1986. *Development of new Survey and Taxonomy for Second Language Learning.* Paper presented at the Learning Strategy Symposium, New York.

———. 1990. *Language Learning Strategies: What Every Teacher Should Know.* New York: Newbury.

———, M. Nyikos, and D. Crookall. 1987. *Learning Strategies of University Foreign Language Students: A Large-Scale Factor Analytic Study.* New York: Newbury.

Patrikis, P. 1988. *Language Learning and Liberal Education.* New Haven, CT: Consortium for Language Teaching and Learning.

Pelling, James and Pamela Pelling. 1974. *Lessons in Ndebele.* London: Longman.

Perrott, D. V. 1950. *Teach Yourself Swahili.* Lincolnwood, IL: Hodder and Stoughton.

Pfister, Guenter G. and Petra Borzilleri. 1977. "Surface Culture Concepts: A Tentative Design for the Evaluation of Cultural Materials in Textbooks." *Die Unterrichtspraxis* 10:102-08.

Pusack, James J. and Sue K. Otto. 1991. "Dear Wilga, Dear Alice, Dear Tracy, Dear Earl: Four Letters on Methodology and Technology." In *Critical Issues in Foreign Language Instruction*, ed. Ellen S. Silber. New York: Garland, 80-103.

————. 1997. "Taking Control of Multimedia." In *Technology Enhanced Language Learning*. ed. Michael D. Bush and Robert M. Terry. Lincolnwood, IL: National Textbook Company, 1-46.

Redden, James, et al. 1963. *Lingala Basic Course*. Washington, D.C.: Foreign Language Institute.

Riordan, J., et al. 1969. *Xhosa Self-Introduction Course*. Port Elizabeth: E.H. Walton.

Rivers, Wilga M. 1981 *Teaching Foreign Language Skills*, 2nd ed. Chicago: U of Chicago P.

————. 1987. *Interactive Language Teaching*. Cambridge: Cambridge UP.

————. 1989a. "Interaction and Communication in the Language Class in an Age of Technology." In *Lessons from the Past with a View Toward the Future*, ed. James E. Alatis. Washington, D.C.: Georgetown UP, 186-197.

————. 1989b. *Ten Principles of Interactive Language Learning and Teaching*. NFLC Occasional Papers. Washington, D.C.: National Foreign Language Center.

Rowlands, E. C. 1969. *Teach Yourself Yoruba*. London: Hodder and Stoughton.

Ruggierp, V. 1988. *The Art of Thinking: A Guide to Critical and Creative Thought*, 2nd ed. New York: Harper & Row.

Safari J. F. 1980. *Swahili Made Easy*. Dar es Salaam: Tanzanian Publishing.

Samarin, William J. 1967. *Basic Course in Sango* Hartford, CT: Hartford Seminary Foundation.

Schleicher, Antonia Y. Folarin. 1993. *Jé K´ Á So Yorubá: Let's Speak Yoruba*. New Haven: Yale UP.

———. 2000. "A Goal-based Approach to African Language Instruction." *Journal of the African Language Teachers Association* 1:25-61.

Searle, D. 1987. "Taking Cues from the Child." In *The Power of Talk.*, ed. C. Staab and S. Hudelson. Unpublished manuscript.

Seelye, H. Ned. 1976. *Teaching Culture: Strategies for Intercultural Communication*. Lincolnwood, IL.: National Textbook Company.

Setukuru, Raymond, et al. 1965. *Kirundi Basic Course*. Washington, D.C.: Foreign Language Institute.

Short, Deborah J. 1994. "Languages Across the Curriculum: Connections with Secondary Language Education." In *Languages Across the Curriculum: Translation Perspectives VII*, ed. H. Stephen Straight. Binghamton: Center for Research in Translation, State U of New York.

Singerman, A., ed. 1988. *Toward a New Integration of Language and Culture*. Northeast Conference Reports. Middlebury, VT: Northeast Conference.

Skinner, Neil. 1973. *Hausa Language Course*. Madison: Department of African Languages and Literatures, University of Wisconsin.

Stempleski, Susan and Barry Tomalin. 1990. *Video in Action*. London: Prentice Hall.

Stempleski, Susan and Paul Arcario, eds. 1992. *Video in Second Language Teaching: Using, Selecting and Producing Video for Classroom Use.* London: Prentice Hall.

Stevick, Earl W. and Olaleye Aremu. 1963. *Yoruba Basic Course.* Washington, D.C.: Foreign Language Institute.

Stevick, Earl W., J. G. Mlela, and F. A. Njenga. 1963. *Swahili Basic Course.* Washington, D.C.: Foreign Language Institute.

Stewart, William, et al. 1966. *Introductory Course in Dakar Wolof.* Washington, D.C.: Center for Applied Linguistics.

Straight, H. Stephen. 1990. "Language Must Be Taught 'Across the Curriculum' to Ensure That Students Develop Functional Skills." *The Chronicle of Higher Education* (March 7):B2.

————, ed. 1994a. *Languages Across the Curriculum: Translation Perspectives VII.* Binghamton: Center for Research in Translation, State U of New York.

————. 1994b. "Some Psycholinguistic Arguments in Favor of the Binghamton LxC Model for Languages Across the Curriculum. In *Languages Across the Curriculum: Transla-tion Perspectives VII*, ed. H. Stephen Straight. Binghamton: Center for Research in Translation, State U of New York.

————, M. G. Rose, and E. H. Badger. 1994. "International Students as Resource Specialists: Binghamton's Language Across the Curriculum Program." In *Languages Across the Curriculum: Translation Perspectives VII*, ed. H. Stephen Straight. Binghamton: Center for Research in Translation, State U of New York., 1-34.

Swift, L.B ., A. Ahaghotu, and E. Ugorji. 1962. *Igbo Basic Course.* Washington, D.C.: Foreign Language Institute.

Swift, Lloyd B., Kalilu Tambadu, and Paul G. Imhoff. 1965. *Fula Basic Course.* Washington, D.C.: Foreign Language Institute.

The Open University. 1981. *Learning from Television: Study Package.* Cambridge, UK: Milton Keynes.

Walton, A Ronald. 1988. "The Case of Chinese." In *ACTFL Proficiency Guidelines of the Less Commonly Taught Languages,* ed. Charles Stansfield and Chip Harman. Washington, D.C.: Center for Applied Linguistics and the American Council on the Teaching of Foreign Languages.

Watkins, Beverly T. 1990. "Program at St. Olaf College Offers Students Incentive to Make Foreign Languages More Than a Requirement." *The Chronicle of Higher Education* (November):28.

Welmers, William E. and Beatrice F. Welmers. 1968. *Igbo A Learner's Manual.* Los Angeles: U of California.

Wesch, M. B. 1994. "Discipline-Based Language Study: Tailored Formats for Diverse Contexts." In *Languages Across the Curriculum: Translation Perspectives VII,* ed. H. Stephen Straight. Binghamton: Center for Research in Translation, State U of New York., 87-100.

Wiley David and David Dwyer. 1980. *African Languages in the 1980s: Direction and Priorities.* East Lansing: Michigan State U African Studies Center.

Wilson, Peter. 1970. *Simplified Swahili.* Nairobi, Kenya: Longman.

Zawawi, Sharifa. 1971. *Kiswahili Kwa Kitendo: An Introductory Course.* New York: Harper and Row.

Index

A

academic background 4, 142
accent 147
adjectives 125, 148
administrative structures 3
adverbs 148
affiliation 1, 9-10
African language: classrooms
51, 114, 135; instruction 2, 25,
28-29, 31, 54-55, 63, 89, 94,
110, 120, 141-142, 169, 175,
211, 216, 226; pedagogy
36-37, 41-42, 46, 53, 120, 134,
153, 189, 196, 207, 210;
textbook 116, 120, 136
African Studies 2, 15-16, 27, 73,
115, 175-176, 180, 188, 197,
216, 219-220, 225, 229
Africanists 157, 187
analytic knowledge 140, 225
Arabic 23, 43, 109, 182, 215
art 73, 102, 140, 152, 226
audio texts 200
authentic: materials 22, 30,
92-93, 98, 103, 105-106,
128-129, 134, 146, 167, 169-2,
174, 178, 199; situations 117,
119

B

background information
144-145, 166
Bambara 116, 179, 185, 205, 220

Brecht and Walton 89, 96,
99-100, 105, 108, 112, 217
bulletin board 168

C

category 3, 5, 21, 39, 196
certification 41, 198
charts 139
Chichewa 116, 123, 205, 225
Chinese 15, 23, 26, 41-42, 182,
184
classroom instruction 60, 130,
161, 163, 198
clientele 15, 20, 29
cognitive development 73
coherent/coherence 19, 64, 67,
72, 82, 143, 180
communicative: activities 49;
competence 30, 48-49, 77, 79,
130, 202; orientation 202-203;
performance 202; skills 73,
84, 161
comprehension 30, 53, 61, 67,
70, 82, 85, 119, 149, 151-152,
164-165, 174
computer 22, 141, 153, 159,
161, 163, 166-169, 203
creativity 62-63, 65, 69, 72-73,
139-140, 144-145, 150-151, 226
credibility 3, 20, 36
critical thinking 71-75, 139,
143, 151, 217-218

function 57, 80, 125, 146, 165, 176, 209
functional approach 48, 91, 95, 103

G

general education information 129
German 11, 19, 23, 46, 90, 93, 181
goals: ALTA 176-179; Center 17, 205-206; conflicting 96; cultural 115, 121-124; educational 112; instructional 125, 130-133, 202; language learning 67, 81; program 6, 13, 15-16, 27, 83, 112, 199, 201; student's/ learner's 62, 64-65, 79, 82, 100-101, 106, 108-109, 111, 204; sub-field 185; teacher's 49, 61, 81
grammar: 20-21, 48-49, 53, 58, 66-67, 73, 80, 119, 124-125, 127, 129, 150, 156, 164, 168, 170, 207; drills 117; driven 21, 95; notes 166; translation exercises 49
grammatical: information 119; notes 97
graphics 164-165

H

Hausa 2, 5, 14, 17, 22, 26, 36, 55-56, 83, 94, 99, 109, 114, 116, 122-123, 163-164, 177-179, 184-185, 189, 205-208, 218, 221, 227
HBCU 5
Hindi 184
history 10, 15-16, 22, 26, 40, 58-59, 78, 94-95, 102-108, 122, 157, 196-197, 203, 221
humanistic 3

I

Igbo 116, 123, 205, 228
impromptu interactions 171
institutional aspects: 1-3, 6-12, 27, 33, 41, 54, 141, 180, 188, 190, 192, 201
instructional: 3, 10, 14, 17-18, 48, 54, 61, 87, 139, 141, 143, 148, 154, 163-164, 166, 178, 203, 211
instructor 4-5, 7-9, 12, 40, 46, 58-60, 74, 96-101, 104-105, 108-110, 112, 135, 137, 147, 152, 155, 160-161, 166, 169, 172-174
integrating video 200

interactive: learning 60, 63-64, 67, 100, 143, 152-153, 155-158, 160; multimedia 155-158, 161-162, 164, 167, 169, 178, 189; program 152-153, 170, 207

intercultural: 21, 227; communicative competence 130

interface 173

intermediate level 6, 17, 23, 51, 53-55, 64, 68, 97, 105, 108, 112, 133, 144, 149-150, 158, 163, 178, 189, 203, 206-207

Internet 22, 160, 167-169, 170, 173-174

intonation 147

J

Japanese 15, 23, 26, 42, 44, 93, 182

K

Kikuyu 2, 116, 202, 205, 216
Kirundi 116, 205, 227
knowledge schema 69
Korean 182, 184

L

language: assessment 200; coordinators 33, 39, 44, 176, 196, 198, 200, 213

Latin 26

learner: achievement 194; outcomes 6, 41

learning: goals 67, 108; styles 100

lecture approach 61

legitimacy 4, 26

lifelong learning 74

Lingala 109, 116, 123, 205-206, 226

linkage 7-9, 12, 14

Luganda 2, 116, 123, 205, 221

M

maps 139

media 22, 131, 133, 148, 167-169, 173, 219

melody 147

metalanguage books 55, 94, 101

model 6, 31, 34, 44, 46, 61-62, 82, 99, 159-160, 171, 205-207, 218, 224, 228

monologues 19, 21

morphological 19

Moshi 1, 19, 22, 29, 39, 167-168, 176, 178, 185, 219, 223